2 to
IN ASIA

THE ITINERARY PLANNER
1993

ROGER RAPOPORT
BURL WILLES

John Muir Publications
Santa Fe, New Mexico

Other books by Roger Rapoport
Is the Library Burning? (with Laurence J. Kirshbaum)
The Great American Bomb Machine
The Superdoctors
The California Catalogue (with Margot Lind)
The Big Player (with Kenneth S. Uston)
California Dreaming: The Political Odyssey of Pat and Jerry Brown
Into the Sunlight: Life After the Iron Curtain

Other JMP travel guidebooks by the authors
Great Cities of Eastern Europe by Roger Rapoport
2 to 22 Days in California by Roger Rapoport
22 Days Around the World by Roger Rapoport and Burl Willes
2 to 22 Days in the Rockies by Roger Rapoport
Undiscovered Islands of the Caribbean, 2nd ed., by Burl Willes
Undiscovered Islands of the Mediterranean, 2nd ed., by Linda Lancione Moyer and Burl Willes
Undiscovered Islands of the U.S. and Canadian West Coast by Linda Lancione Moyer and Burl Willes

John Muir Publications, P.O. Box 613, Santa Fe, NM 87504

© 1989, 1991, 1992, by RDR Syndicate
Cover and maps © 1989, 1991, 1992, by John Muir Publications
All rights reserved.
Printed in the United States of America

ISSN 1062-4325
ISBN 1-56261-055-4

Distributed to the book trade by
W.W. Norton & Company, Inc.
New York, New York

Cover Photo Leo de Wys Inc./Steve Vidler
Design Mary Shapiro
Maps Holly Wood
Typography Copygraphics, Inc., Santa Fe, NM
Printer McNaughton & Gunn, Inc.

CONTENTS

Acknowledgments		v
How to Use this Book		1
Itinerary		16
Day 1	United States to Kyoto	21
Day 2	Kyoto: Philosopher's Trail and Shijo Street	27
Day 3	Kyoto: Ryoanji, Kinkakuji, and Imperial Palace	34
Day 4	Kyoto: Shugakuin, Heian Shrine, and Kiyomizu Temple	38
Day 5	Kyoto to Beijing	44
Day 6	Beijing: The Great Wall and Tian'anmen Square	52
Day 7	Beijing: The Forbidden City	56
Day 8	Beijing to Shanghai	60
Day 9	Shanghai: The Bund, Yuyuan Garden, and Shanghai Museum	65
Day 10	Suzhou	69
Day 11	Shanghai: People's Park and Children's Palaces	73
Day 12	Shanghai to Hong Kong	76
Day 13	Hong Kong: Victoria Peak, Stanley, and Shek-O	83
Day 14	Hong Kong: Outer Islands	88
Day 15	Hong Kong: The Land Between	93
Days 16 to 22: Option A	Thailand	98
Days 16 to 22: Option B	Bali	128
Posttour Option	Hawaii	159
Index		163

ACKNOWLEDGMENTS

Derk and Robin Richardson revisited our favorite haunts in Thailand, making many new discoveries of their own. After many hard days in the Southeast Asian office, they returned to write those sections of the book. Linda Lancione Moyer did a fine job researching the Kyoto section. To all of them, thanks and a tip of the 22-Day hat.

The tourist offices of Japan, Hong Kong, Indonesia, and Thailand were all helpful, as were the China International Travel Service and the Hawaii Visitors Bureau. In particular, we'd like to acknowledge the assistance of Catherine Remedios, Peter Beren, Judith Lubman, Stan Sesser, and, of course, the entire staff at John Muir Publications.

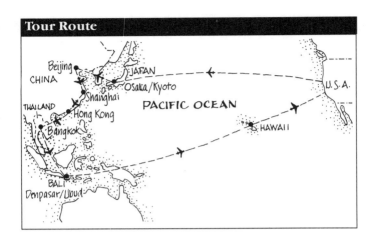

HOW TO USE THIS BOOK

A dream 22-day trip to Asia will cost less than a comparable visit to Europe. While the prices are modest, you'll be able to see some of the world's most exotic locales without sacrificing quality or comfort. You won't have to worry about standing in line or, with rare exceptions, making hotel reservations months in advance. As you circle the Pacific you'll be traveling in some of the safest countries in the world, enjoying the best restaurants, and exploring cultures where civilization flourished at a time when Paris and London were miserable medieval slums. This proven itinerary will ease your way through the many splendors of Japan, China, Hong Kong, Thailand, and Bali.

After more than twenty trips to Asia, including six to research this book, we believe there has never been a better time to visit this region. Who are we to make this claim? Burl is a veteran travel agent who has visited more than 100 countries; Roger is the author of 2 to 22 Days Guides to California and the Rockies. We frequently recommend this itinerary with impressive results. The typical first-time visitor comes home already thinking about his or her next trip. Our suggestions, endorsed and augmented by the experiences of many clients and readers, are yours to enjoy. While this book is designed for the independent traveler, it can also be useful for someone on a tour who wants to break away and enjoy some of the special finds often overlooked by large groups.

Although it's easy to generalize about the magic of Asia, we believe the small details covered in this itinerary, like a bike tour route for Suzhou or a particular *warung* (food concession) on our restaurant map of Ubud, Bali, are crucial to the success of your trip. In many cases, you will find proprietors of inns in places like Kyoto or Chiang Mai almost as fascinating as the attractions you have traveled thousands of miles to see. But don't just take our word for it. Use this book as a template for one of the most memorable trips of your life. Adapt it to your special interests and time limitations. If you have less than 22 days, pick the most intriguing destinations and save the rest for a later trip. If you have extra time, follow our suggestions for itinerary extensions.

This book concentrates on the highlights of Japan, China, Hong Kong, Thailand, and Bali in a workable itinerary designed to help you experience the sights and sounds of each culture without rushing from city to city in a futile attempt to see everything. To make your trip more rewarding, we've divided this book into daily itinerary sections, containing:

1. A **general overview** of each day.

2. **Suggested schedules** for travel, sightseeing, shopping, and meals.

3. Summaries of major **sightseeing highlights** (rated ▲▲▲ Don't miss; ▲▲ Try hard to see; ▲ Worthwhile if you can make it), with step-by-step walking tours and excursion directions to the most important sights.

4. **Food** and **accommodations** suggestions, from bargain and moderately priced favorites to deluxe splurges.

5. **Practical tips**—random tidbits that will help make your trip go well.

6. **Itinerary options**—excursion suggestions for travelers who have more time.

7. **Maps** designed to show you walking routes and how to find recommended restaurants and sightseeing highlights.

Why Asia?

Choosing a vacation destination is a delicate balancing act. Perhaps you're the kind of person who is happiest exploring the heart of a great metropolis. Or you may prefer to spend an afternoon with a secluded beach to yourself. Exotic dishes served at modest prices are always a temptation. And who can resist a chance to visit great temples, world famous landmarks, or the inner sanctums of legendary dynasties?

Thanks to bargain Circle Pacific Fares, it is possible to create the Asian vacation of a lifetime in just 22 days. This

How to Use this Book 3

book, an East Asian sampler, takes you to the very best of a region that is a perennial favorite among world travelers. If you've never been to Asia, you'll see why it is so popular as soon as you arrive at your first stop, Japan's ancient imperial capital, Kyoto. If you have been to Asia before, this book offers many compelling reasons to return.

When we recommend Asia, people often ask us, "Why now?" Some of the reasons are obvious. As *2 to 22 Days in Asia* demonstrates, Asia is a truly blessed region for the traveler, filled with one-of-a-kind treasures and destinations, a mecca for students of art, history, architecture, design, and religion. The magic of a Chinese garden, the Balinese Peliatan Legong dancers, and a Thai elephant procession represent only a few of the surprises you'll find along this 22-day route.

We urge you to go soon, because the Asia we love is changing rapidly. Some of the changes, such as the Chinese takeover of Hong Kong, have already been mandated. Others, such as the modernization of some of Asia's greatest cultural centers, are the inevitable by-product of twentieth-century progress. At a time when so many cities in Asia and the rest of the world are trying to use Los Angeles as a growth model, your visit creates an economic incentive to protect ancient temples, palaces, and scenic areas. For example, nature-conscious visitors provide a good reason to keep proposed chemical plants away from the coral reef sanctuaries of the Phuket Coast. Your very presence pleads the case for the old Asia of teak forests, seventeenth-century monasteries, and time warps like Shanghai's Huangpu River Bund.

Your reward for a long journey is one of the world's great travel bargains. Happily, this is not one of those books that saves you a few dollars by sticking you in some mildewy room in the middle of nowhere. You will enjoy some of the best bargains of a lifetime: fine inns for as little as $5 a night, including breakfast, airfares that are perhaps the greatest value in the transportation industry, and memorable ferry rides through one of the world's most beautiful harbors for as little as $2.

These are some of the reasons why Asia has lured us back many times and why, after exploring the length and breadth of this land, we have recommended as your ultimate travel destinations Japan, Hong Kong, the People's Republic of China, Thailand, and Indonesia. Within each of these nations, we have recommended our favorite excursions, shrines, beaches, neighborhood walks, inns, restaurants, and shops. Besides field-testing this route ourselves, we have introduced it to many of our friends, who have returned with rave reviews. In the Kyoto section, we will share with you our favorite small hotel in the world, a quiet Japanese inn with affordable rates which makes Kyoto a "must" first stop in Asia.

Your next stop, the People's Republic of China, is easily accessible to independent travelers. You'll have time to discover the Middle Kingdom on your own instead of being herded about in a large tour group that wastes hours at interminable meals arranged by tour guides who pocket handsome tips from restaurant owners. On your self-guided trip, you'll have time to leisurely explore Beijing's Summer Palace, the classic gardens of Suzhou, and the traditional neighborhoods skipped by the official government-led tours.

Hong Kong is the most dramatically situated city in Asia, surrounded by breathtaking bays, mountains, and islands. Hong Kong's intensity and excitement are not to be missed. Only a few miles away you'll see remnants of ancient China on more secluded islands and in the uncrowded New Territories.

Instead of trying to include both Thailand and Indonesia in a single trip, we recommend that you choose one of these countries and see it more thoroughly.

Thailand's colorful temples, outstanding beaches, and fascinating wildlife make it one of Asia's most popular destinations. You'll ride an elephant in the hill country, sample exotic foods in Bangkok, and snorkel in translucent waters off one of Thailand's hundred-plus tropical islands.

Bali, Indonesia's predominantly Hindu island, is one of the most exotic destinations in the world. Should you decide to visit Indonesia, you will easily succumb to the artistic batiks, wood-carved masks, clothes, jewelry, and paintings at bargain prices. You'll experience a colorful Hindu festival or dance, discover mountain villages and terraced rice fields, and still have time to snorkel, swim, or walk on a long, secluded beach before your journey home.

This book recommends accommodations in all price ranges, from hostels and inns for a few dollars a day to the most luxurious hotels in the world. We have personally tried all the lodgings we recommend in this book, as well as the reasonably priced local restaurants, popular for their culinary traditions and, in several cases, for their unique locations.

Getting There

The competition among the airlines flying to Asia means incredible bargains for the traveler. Airfares as low as 4 cents per mile do not mean cutbacks on service or reliability. Japan Airlines, Cathay Pacific, Singapore Air Lines, and Thai Airways are favorite airlines of the well traveled for their comfort, in-flight services, and cuisine. Other choices, also excellent, using wide-bodied, comfortable 747s and DC10s, include Garuda Indonesian, Malaysian, Canadian, United, China, Japan, and Northwest airlines.

Full-price Circle Pacific Economy Fares that include Japan, China, Hong Kong, and Bangkok start at $1,500 in low season from the U.S. West Coast. If you choose Bali instead of Bangkok, the full fare will be about $2,000. Add $100 to $200 if you are leaving from the East Coast. Add about $1,500 if you are traveling in business class. Keep in mind that there is wide variation in pricing depending on carrier and time of departure. Of course, if you are only traveling to one or two of the destinations recommended in this itinerary, your fare will be significantly less. Be sure to shop prices with a number of different carriers. When you purchase a ticket to your farthest destination, you get two free stopovers.

Using the most direct routing on Japan Airlines or CAAC, you fly directly from Osaka to Beijing. United and Northwest provide similar service but require you to connect to China via Tokyo. Your intra-China legs to Shanghai and on to Hong Kong may be included in the ticket, depending on the carrier and the type of fare. If your intra-China flights from Beijing to Shanghai and Hong Kong are not part of the Circle Pacific Fare, plan to add another $225. The Yogyakarta extension to Java is free if you use a circle fare with Garuda Indonesian. Allow $150 round-trip for flying the Bangkok-Chiang Mai side trip in Thailand.

Most good travel agents who do substantial business in Asia can get you a better deal through a wholesaler, known in the trade as a consolidator. This will bring the price down considerably. Some agencies that specialize in low fares (as well as discounts in business and first class) publish ads in papers like the *Village Voice* and the *New York Times* in the East and the *San Francisco Examiner-Chronicle* and the *Los Angeles Times* in the West. All accredited travel agents are bonded, while some consolidators are not. If you buy directly from a consolidator, you shouldn't pay until you receive your ticket.

Trip cancellation insurance is always a good idea, especially if you're using discount fares. Excellent information on this subject is available in the January 1989 issue of *Consumer Reports Travel Letter*, available for $5 from CRTL, 2506 Washington Street, Mt. Vernon, NY 10553.

In general, the lower-cost Circle Pacific Fares may require you to use connecting flights to some of the destinations on this itinerary. You may find that there's an extra charge to take advantage of nonstop routings. For example, only United offers nonstop service from San Francisco to Osaka, your Day 1 destination. As we've previously mentioned, on the Osaka-Beijing leg both CAAC and ANA offer nonstop service. The added fare, if any, may be well worth the convenience. If you choose the Thailand option, there is direct service back to San Francisco on United or Northwest. Garuda offers direct service from Bali back to Los Angeles. Should you choose to stop over in Hawaii on your way home, you'll find good connections on United, Northwest, Japan Air Lines, or Garuda.

Make your airline reservations as far in advance as possible. Asia flights are always heavily booked, especially around Christmas and in June, July, and August when Asians come to the United States. You should not begin your trip without hotel reservations during Christmas holidays, October and April for Japan, or Chinese New Year (mid-February) for Hong Kong.

Is Asia Safe?
Japan and China are two of the safest countries for tourists in the world. In Kyoto there is so little crime that some shopkeepers do not bring their merchandise in at night or bother to lock their doors! Thailand and Bali are also extremely safe, but travelers should be advised that a possession that attracts the eye may be "borrowed indefinitely," so it is wise to watch your cameras, radios, jewelry, and articles of clothing.

Take your money in the form of a well-known brand of traveler's checks. The exchange rate for them is usually more favorable than for cash. You'll find currency exchange banks at all major international airports. Credit cards can be used at most major hotels, many restaurants, and some stores.

Money
We quote prices in this book in the local currency of each country, followed in parentheses by approximate U.S. dollar values. These prices change constantly, of course, due to inflation and changes in international currency exchange rates. You're likely to find that prices in some countries have remained roughly the same in the local currency while the U.S. dollar prices have changed; in other countries along your route, prices in local currency will have changed while U.S. dollar prices remain fairly accurate. Despite such changes, the prices we quote here will give you a good idea of relative values within each

country. The approximate foreign currency exchange rates as of mid-1991 are:
   Japan: 1 yen (Y1) = $.0076; $1 = Y131.
   China: 1 yuan (Y1) = $.19; $1 = Y5.3.
   Hong Kong: 1 Hong Kong dollar (HK$1) = $.13; $1 = HK$7.8.
   Thailand: 1 baht = $.04; $1 = 25.3 baht.
   Bali: 1 rupiah = $.00053; $1 = 1,900 rupiah.

Lodging

The Japanese are meticulous housekeepers, and if you stay at a hostel ($10 a day), Buddhist temple ($26), or Japanese-style inn ($60 and up), you can be assured of a quiet, clean room and gracious, polite hospitality. Westerners who travel independently in Japan are very rare; you will be treated with awe, respect, and much kindness.

In Hong Kong, the busy and well-located YMCA International Hotel faces the ferry terminal. Rates here start at $10 for a dormitory room, $50 for a pleasant room in a modern high-rise with private bath, and $80 for the family suite with kitchen. Comfortable midrange hotels start around $60 to $80. Traveling deluxe ($150 and up), you will be pampered by huge staffs at the finest hotels in the world.

In the People's Republic of China, allow $50 to $60 for a moderate room and $100 and up for a Western-style hotel room with all amenities (room service, telephone, air-conditioning). Low occupancy rates have led to last-minute reduction of hotel rates in cities like Beijing and Shanghai. You may find it possible to ask for, and get, significant discounts in major Chinese cities. Inquire when you arrive.

In both Thailand and Bali, the graciousness of the people is felt, whether at $10-a-night beachfront cottages in Thailand or $8-a-night homestays on Bali. Western-style toilets and showers are the rule in moderate to luxury categories ($30-$300) but not so in budget accommodations, where floor toilets and bucket showers are the rule.

Food

Japanese food is a work of art; much time and thought goes into its preparation and presentation. Wax models of meals are displayed in windows, often with prices attached. Continental breakfast is often included in the price of lodging. Lunch specials of sushi, tofu, noodles, or spaghetti are $8 to $10. One can picnic for lunch (allow $5), finding bargains in the local market (in-season fruit, produce, sandwiches).

Hong Kong is a gourmet paradise; food of every type and description is available at small restaurants ($10-$15) or in luxury restaurants with unique waterfront vistas.

In the People's Republic of China, a Chinese-style breakfast of rice and soup is delicious and less expensive than Western-style food. Allow $20 to $30 a day for Western-style food, less if you eat at small shops and stay away from hotel dining rooms.

Thai food is always fresh and generally spicy. Tropical fruits abound and are very inexpensive. Moderately priced meals are $3 to $8 and deluxe meals $15 to $25.

On Bali, the food is less spicy and even less expensive. Fried rice, noodles, and *gado gado* (hot vegetable salad with peanut dressing) cost $1 to $3. At deluxe hotels, allow $10 to $20 for an excellent meal.

Public Transportation

In Japan, buses are frequent, efficient, and reasonably priced ($2). Drivers do not speak English but are helpful if you have your destination written in Japanese characters. If you prefer taxis, you'll be treated to the best in the world at prices that will not break your budget; suggested short trips in the itinerary average $10 to $20 each.

In Hong Kong, the ferry system is one of the best in the world. Travel to offshore islands and nearby towns costs less than $2. Within the city, the subway is efficient, safe, easy to use, and inexpensive.

In China, the buses are crowded and not very comfortable, so you may decide to rent a bicycle in Suzhou ($3-$5 per day). Local taxis average $2 to $4 per trip.

Bus travel in Thailand is efficient and inexpensive. However, we find trains preferable for ground transit. For local trips within the cities, taxis are very reasonable.

On Bali, *bemos*, small public vans that carry five to eight passengers, are omnipresent and can take you wherever you want to go for minuscule sums. Private taxis can be hired by the hour or day at approximately $5 per hour.

Visas

A valid passport is necessary for travel anywhere in Asia. You will need a visa for the People's Republic of China. Unless you have an invitation to visit (you would then apply to an embassy), you can obtain your application and process your visa through one of the visa services mentioned below. A visa is no longer necessary for travel to Japan, and no visas are required for Hong Kong, Thailand (for stays less than 15 days), or Indonesia (for stays less than 60 days).

An easy way to obtain visas is to take advantage of a visa service. The very nominal extra charge is justified by the fast service and convenience. Two excellent companies we've used are Visas Unlimited (582 Market St., San Francisco, CA 94105; tel. 415-495-5216) and Visa Aides (870 Market St., San Francisco, CA 95105; tel. 415-362-7137). Visa service companies are listed in most telephone yellow pages under Passport Photo and Visa Services.

When to Go

The best months to start this itinerary are late October, November, and January to May.

July, August, and September are very hot, rainy months for Japan, Hong Kong, China, and Thailand. Bali, below the equator, is less hot and less rainy then. November is Bali's hottest month and December the rainiest. Kyoto, Japan, is cold in winter (December through February) but rarely gets snow. The cold is offset by the lack of crowds at all tourist spots, temples, and gardens.

Health Precautions

We recommend that you heed your physician's advice on vaccinations, immunizations, and other precautions against malaria, hepatitis, venereal diseases, cholera, and typhoid fever. Your physician may also suggest medicine to take with you for a flulike cold that often strikes down travelers in China, especially in winter.

We are strong believers in preventative medicine on Asian trips. We always drink bottled water, beer, wine, or soft drinks rather than tap water. We avoid shellfish and raw food and prefer to carry our own chopsticks to use when eating any freshly cooked food from street stalls.

Chances of getting malaria or dengue fever are minimal with protection against disease-carrying mosquitoes. Use an insect repellent containing Deet. Be sure to protect your ankles, a prime mosquito target. At night, sleep under a mosquito net or fan if you are in an area where mosquitoes are prevalent.

If you are concerned about the possibility of being treated in a foreign hospital, why not buy a medical evacuation policy from a company like Travel Assistance International (800-368-7878)? Their policies give you 24-hour coverage in the event of illness. If you need treatment, you will immediately be transported at their expense to a hospital with English-speaking staff. Or, if necessary, you will be flown home for care. The policy can also pay to have a relative flown over to assist you on the trip home. By the way, do not forget to bring all your prescriptions with you.

Pack and Take

TRAVEL LIGHT! Ideally, take carryon baggage. You'll save time at your destination and often be one of the first through customs and immigration. Even more important, you'll eliminate the possibility of delayed or lost luggage and much inconvenience. Never check anything you can't travel without (glasses, credit cards, medicine, address book), and it never hurts to carry your passport, airline tickets, and traveler's checks in a money belt. Photocopy your passport and airline ticket (first page of each) and pack the copies separately.

Clothing

Wear your warm outfit on the plane—a sweater and a jacket, if you are leaving in winter. A small portable umbrella can be useful in any month, especially when you are traveling with few changes of clothing. Lightweight rubber overshoes will keep your walking shoes dry during the rainy days. For the tropics, light cotton clothing is ideal. Women can buy a sarong to use as a skirt, but cotton shorts and pants are acceptable nearly everywhere. There's no need to take more than one pair of comfortable, all-purpose walking shoes, but do take a pair of rubber thongs or sandals for Thailand and Bali. Include a bathing suit, two light shirts, and shorts. Don't worry if you feel you haven't packed enough. In Thailand or Bali, you'll find everything you need and more at very reasonable prices.

Even if you travel light, you'll still find certain items essential: an alarm clock, an eye mask, dark glasses, ear plugs, a pencil-size flashlight, and reading material. Bring antibacterial ointment, Band-Aids, prescription drugs, vitamins, sunscreen, and mosquito repellent.

Recommended Reading

Japan: The best general information book on Japan is *Japan: A Traveler's Companion* by Lensey Namioka (New York: Vanguard Press). *Travel Guide Kyoto* (Tokyo: Japan Travel Bureau) is a small, useful book with more details on our recommended sights. It's worth taking along.

A Guide to the Gardens of Kyoto by Marc Trieb and Ron Herman (Tokyo: Shufunotomo Company, Ltd.) is a loving introduction to the subtleties of Japanese landscaping as well as a detailed appreciation of the individual temples and palace gardens. *Old Kyoto: A Guide to Tradi-*

tional Shops, Restaurants, and Inns (Tokyo and New York: Kodansha International) and *Kyoto: Seven Paths to the Heart of the City* (Tokyo and New York: Kodansha International), both by Diana Durston, reveal out-of-the-way places, timeless neighborhoods, and traditions and will give you a sense of the life of the city away from the beaten tourist path. The second has magnificent color photos. If you have more time in Japan, we recommend another book in the 22 Days series, *22 Days in Japan* by David Old (Santa Fe, N.M.: John Muir Publications).

China: For an excellent introduction to modern China before you go, read Paul Theroux's *Riding the Iron Rooster* (New York: Putnam). The description of his year-long train ride through the Middle Kingdom is not to be missed. Also recommended are *Red Star over China* by Edgar Snow (New York: Grove Press) and Fox Butterfield's *China: Alive in the Bitter Sea* (New York: Bantam).

Another excellent book is Pan Ling's *In Search of Old Shanghai* (Hong Kong: Joint Publishing Co.). This is a perfect traveling companion while exploring China's largest city. Also worth taking along is *22 Days in China* by Gaylon Duke and Zenia Victor (Santa Fe, N.M.: John Muir Publications).

You may want to gather relevant material from a number of other excellent books before leaving. Among them is *China: A Travel Survival Kit* (Oakland: Lonely Planet). China Books and Periodicals in San Francisco offers many useful titles, including *Shopping in China* by Roberta Stalberg and *Magnificent China: A Guide to Its Cultural Treasure* by Kuan and Kuan.

Indonesia: *Island of Bali* by Miguel Covarrubias (New York: KPI), written in 1938 and recently republished, is a classic work that evokes the magic of Bali and is in no way outdated. If you read only one book on Bali, it should be this one.

Bali and Lombok: A Travel Survival Kit (Oakland: Lonely Planet) and *Bali Insight Guide* (Singapore: APA Productions HK, Ltd.) are both excellent general information reading. Also recommended is Bill Dalton's *Indonesia Handbook* (Chico, Calif.: Moon Publications).

Thailand: *Chiang Mai and North Thailand* by John Hoskin (Hong Kong: Hong Kong Publishing Company) is worth reading if you plan to spend more time in the Hill Country. This area is also covered in the *Insight Guide Thailand* (Singapore: APA Productions HK Ltd.). You'll also find Derk Richardson's *2 to 22 Days in Thailand* (Santa Fe, N.M.: John Muir Publications) valuable. He researched the Thailand section of this book.

Tourist Boards

For additional background on the countries covered in this book, contact the official government tourist organizations or, in the case of China, the travel service:

Japan National Tourist Organization, 630 Fifth Avenue, New York, NY 10111, (212) 757-5640; or 360 Post Street, San Francisco, CA 94108, (415) 989-7140.

China International Travel Service, 60 E. 42nd Street, Suite 465, New York, NY 10165, (212) 867-0271.

Hong Kong Tourist Association, 333 N. Michigan Avenue, Suite 2323, Chicago, IL 60601-3966, (312) 782-3872.

Tourism Authority of Thailand, 3440 Wilshire Boulevard, Suite 1101, Los Angeles, CA 90010, (213) 382-2353.

Indonesia Tourist Promotion Office, 3457 Wilshire Boulevard, Los Angeles, CA 90010, (213) 387-2078.

Please Note

You've probably been told that the more things change, the more they stay the same. Not true in Asia. On arrival at each destination, we urge you to supplement this book with a good local map. Museum and attraction hours and routings are, of course, subject to change. We do not recommend driving in any of the countries covered in this itinerary (with the exception of our Hawaii option). You will find local transit, cabs, and hired drivers the best ways to get around. Check the weather forecast before setting out for rural areas. Prices listed in this book are approximate, subject to change and currency fluctuations, and of course, inflation Because the least expensive rooms tend to be booked first, you may be quoted a higher rate. Trip cancellation insurance is always a good idea. Check with your travel agent for details. Before leaving the United States it's a good idea to call the U.S. State Department in Washington or your local passport office to review any citizen's travel advisories. The U.S. embassies and consulates along the way are also a good resource for information on areas that are considered unsafe for tourism in Asia or anywhere else in the world. In general we do not recommend massage parlors or bars outside of major tourist hotels. We welcome your comments and suggestions; write to us in care of the publisher.

ITINERARY

DAY 1 Depart for Osaka, connect to the historic capital city of Kyoto, and check into your inn or hotel, where you can relax in a warm Japanese bath before heading out for dinner at a rotating sushi bar or vegetarian restaurant.

DAY 2 Walk the Philosopher's Trail, Kyoto's Zen main line. Shop on bustling Shijo Street, try your hand at a game of pachinko, and sample nightlife in the Gion district.

DAY 3 Visit two of Kyoto's best-known temples, Ryoanji and Kinkakuji, tour the Imperial Palace or the shogun's domain at Nijo Castle, and attend a show featuring traditional Japanese performing arts at Gion Corner.

DAY 4 Tour the imperial villa, Shugakuin, picnic at Heian Shrine, and hike up to Kiyomizu Temple before returning to the Kyoto Handicraft Center to shop for Japanese crafts, including silk kimonos and fine porcelain.

DAY 5 Fly to Beijing, check into a hotel room overlooking the Forbidden City, and explore the shops of Wangfujing Street. After a Szechuan dinner and a visit to the night market, have a nightcap at the Beijing Hotel.

DAY 6 Ascend the meticulously restored Great Wall at Badaling, one of the wonders of the world. Visit the Ming Tombs and the giant stone menagerie guarding the Sacred Way. Back in town you'll visit the birthplace of the People's Republic, Tiananmen Square, enjoy a Peking duck dinner, and watch an evening performance at the Dazhalan Acrobatics Theater.

DAY 7 Your morning is devoted to exploring portions of the 9,000-room Forbidden City, followed by a noon visit to the Temple of Heaven, one of the country's greatest architectural achievements. The afternoon is reserved for the Summer Palace the imperial family's 700-acre retreat,

Itinerary

where you can lunch at the Listening to the Orioles restaurant, explore a 10-story temple, or paddle about like royalty on Kunming Lake.

DAY 8 After a morning visit to Lama Temple, home of the Buddhas of the Three Ages, you'll fly to Shanghai and check into the Peace Hotel. Following dinner, enjoy a performance by the hotel's legendary jazz band, back in action after a 27-year government ban on Western jazz performances.

DAY 9 Today you'll stroll Asia's most famous promenade, Shanghai's Bund. Your walk along the Huangpu waterfront leads to Yuyuan Garden and the Wuxingting Teahouse. In the afternoon visit the city's Museum of Art and History. After dinner enjoy the renowned Shanghai Acrobatic Theater.

DAY 10 An hour-long train ride takes you to the Grand Canal town of Suzhou, home of some of China's greatest gardens. You'll visit such classics as the Humble Administrator's Garden and the Surging Wave Pavilion before catching your train back to Shanghai.

DAY 11 Stroll Shanghai's leading shopping street, Nanjing Road, to People's Park. After a midday visit to the Jade Buddha Temple, see some of the city's most talented young people perform at the Municipal Children's Palace.

DAY 12 Fly to Hong Kong, check into your hotel, explore the crown colony's colorful bazaars and dine at one of dozens of restaurants on Causeway Bay's Food Street. Ride through the bustling harbor on the Star Ferry and take the tram to the top of Victoria Peak for a panoramic view of this Asian citadel.

DAY 13 Explore lesser-known Hong Kong Island. Take the tram to the top of Victoria Peak and walk down the mountain's backside to Pokfulam Reservoir. After lunch at Repulse Bay, shop for designer label bargains in Stanley and then catch a cab to Shek-O to sample Chinese village life before riding back to bustling Hong Kong Central.

DAY 14 See the Hong Kong most visitors miss by ferrying to one of three fascinating outer islands, Cheung Chau, Lamma, or Lantau. Lunch at a monastery, swim at scenic beaches, cycle through farm and fishing villages, visit temples, or hike verdant peaks to enjoy the views. This is a delightful way to turn back the clock in the Hong Kong archipelago, and the ferry tab will only set you back a couple of dollars.

DAY 15 Get a preview of the colony's future by visiting the New Territories spread out along the Chinese border. You'll tour the Bamboo Forest Monastery, visit a traditional market, see farms tended by black-hatted Hakka women, and visit a local bird sanctuary. You can also enjoy a picturesque ferry ride through the fjordlike scenery of Tolo Harbour or, if you prefer, shop for bargains at some of the city's factory outlets.

OPTION A: THAILAND

DAY 16 Fly to Bangkok, Asia's most exotic city, where a jet boat whisks you to the Grand Palace and the Temple of the Emerald Buddha. Continue to Wat Po, home of the Temple of the Reclining Buddha. Dine on inexpensive fresh seafood and fine curries before sampling the city's legendary nightlife.

DAY 17 Your morning begins with a cruise to Wat Arun, the Temple of Dawn. After visiting this landmark, distinguished by its 282-foot-tall central spire, you'll visit the handsome Royal Barges.

DAY 18 Fly to Chiang Mai, your base for a trip to the northern hill country. Explore the city and line up your trek or tour for the following day. Dinner at the Diamond Hotel's teak mansion.

Itinerary

DAY 19 Create your own personalized tour from a fascinating array of choices. You'll be able to visit traditional tribal villages and the ancient capital of Chiang Rai. Alternatively, you can go for a hill country elephant ride, cruise the Mekong River by longtail boat, or hike a jungle trail, where it's easy to cool off in the spray of a waterfall.

DAY 20 Explore Chiang Mai's finest temples, such as Wat Chiang Man, Wat Phra Singh, and Wat Phrathat. Tour handicraft workshops and shop for lacquerware, wood carvings, silverware, jewelry, parasols, and celadon pottery. After dinner enjoy the carnival atmosphere of the night bazaar, where you can continue to shop, sample delicacies from the food stalls, listen to music, and kibitz.

DAY 21 Fly south to Koh Samui Island on the Gulf of Thailand, check into an inexpensive bungalow, and hit the beach—a perfect place for snorkeling, scuba diving, and sunbathing.

DAY 22 Another day of R and R on the beach, along with a chance to see some of the island's landmarks, such as the Big Buddha at Hin Ngu Temple. Or travel up into the jungle to see the picturesque waterfalls at Na Muang and Hin Lad.

OPTION B: BALI

DAY 16 Fly to Denpasar, Bali, transfer to Ubud, and check into your hotel.

DAY 17 Explore Ubud, one of Asia's most remarkable villages. Shop for shadow puppets, paintings, wind chimes, fine fabrics, masks, or wood carvings. Visit the Puri Lukisan Museum and Puri Saren, the home of Prince Cokorda Agung. In the evening, attend a Balinese dance performance accompanied by a gamelan band.

DAY 18 Walk along Campuhan Ridge, see the stone carvings at Goa Gajah's elephant cave entrance and the friezes of Yeh Pulu. In Mas, you'll find some of the island's best mask makers and wood carvers. Attend another evening dance performance.

DAY 19 Explore the northern highlands and jungles on a trip to Lake Bratan, with stops at a monkey forest, temples, flower market, and botanical garden. Relax on Lovina Beach, which offers some of the island's best snorkeling. Return to Ubud via Kupu Kupu Barong to enjoy one of the island's most memorable panoramas.

DAY 20 Drive through villages famous for their gold and silver craftsmanship en route to the oceanfront temple of Tanah Lot, an island landmark. Enjoy a special Balinese dinner at Satri's in Ubud.

DAY 21 See Bali's spiritual heartland on a drive to Gunung Kawi, Batur, and the island's mother temple at Besakih. Like the pilgrims who come here regularly, you'll visit some of the 30 temple buildings that are the site of holy purification ceremonies. In the afternoon you'll check into an inn or hotel at Candi Dasa, a relaxing and hassle-free alternative to the jammed beaches to the southwest at Kuta and Sanur.

DAY 22 Snorkel off Balina Beach for a look at marine life and coral formations in the warm Indonesian waters. Or, if you're feeling ambitious, sign up for a diving trip to your choice of seven excellent sites off the Balinese coast.

ITINERARY EXTENSIONS: Yogyakarta/Borobudur

POSTTOUR OPTION: Hawaii

DAY 1
UNITED STATES TO KYOTO

Begin your trip to Asia with a long flight to Osaka. Crossing the international date line, you will arrive in the late afternoon or early evening as the sun casts its last shadows over the magical city of Kyoto. The restful and serene atmosphere of your hotel will mean a comfortable first night in Asia.

Suggested Schedule

Morning	Depart for Osaka.
Late afternoon	Arrive at Osaka International Airport.
5:00 p.m.	Customs, immigration.
5:30 p.m.	Take bus to Kyoto train station.
6:30 p.m.	Taxi from train station to hotel.
7:00 p.m.	Short walk in neighborhood, dinner.
8:00 p.m.	Early to bed.

Arrival

Fly to Osaka directly or via Tokyo's Narita Airport. After customs inspection and immigration, obtain local currency and coins at the bank near the exit door. Rates here are comparable to Kyoto banks, so you may want to purchase enough for your entire stay. For a quick mental conversion from yen to dollars, multiply the yen amount by 7.6 and then move the decimal point over three places. For example, 1,000 yen is worth about $7.60. Once outside the airport, turn left and walk 500 feet to the bus area. The bus for Kyoto will have a sign in English on the front window. Purchase your ticket from a nearby machine by inserting Y830 ($6.30) and pressing the button marked "Kyoto" in English. The ride takes approximately 60 minutes. Get off at the railway station, where you will see a line of taxis to take you to your hotel.

Cabs are plentiful and can be hailed as in most Western countries. The flat starting fare of Y420 ($3.25) will cover a short trip. It is likely that the driver won't recognize your pronunciation of your destination, so point the

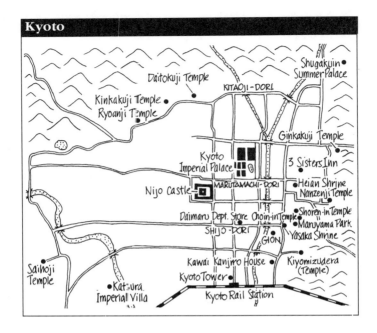

Japanese characters out to him on a map or carry the name and address written in Japanese. Tipping is expected only when you have luggage.

Luggage will probably go in the car with you. The trunk is reserved for the feather duster and polishing rags. This is a country with a lot of car pride; the cab seats are covered with white lace, and the drivers wear white gloves and sometimes chauffeur's caps. Cab doors are controlled by the driver; you're not supposed to touch them.

Helpful Hints

At least one Western-style toilet can often be found in public places, usually labeled in English "Western lavatory" or "foreigner's lavatory." Just as you take off your shoes before entering a house, temple, or traditional restaurant, so you sometimes must wear special slippers provided at the entrance to the toilet and washing areas.

The traditional Japanese bath is a deep tub of very hot water for soaking, in which soap and washcloth are not used. You are requested to do your washing and rinsing in the shower before entering the tub.

Accommodations
Most accommodations we list below are near the Heian Shrine, with easy access to many of the major tourist attractions.

Dormitory-style hostels, beginning at Y1,400 ($10.65) per person, provide the least expensive accommodations in Kyoto. Any Japan National Tourist Office can provide you with a list of hostels in Kyoto and the rest of the country, along with booking information. If you are a member of a Youth Hostels Association that belongs to the International Youth Hostel Federation, your membership card with the correct year label admits you. Otherwise you can apply for an International Guest Card for Y2,200 ($17). Apply to Youth Hostels Inc., Hoken Kaikan, 1-2 Sadohara-cho, Icxhigaya, Shinjuku-ku, Tokyo 162; (03) 269-5831.

Some Buddhist temples in Japan offer overnight accommodations to visitors of all faiths. **Myokenji Temple** in Kyoto is open to visitors all year, with small, traditionally furnished guest rooms and toilet and bath facilities down the hall. Each room either looks out on a garden or has a flower arrangement to aid meditation. (Myokenji Temple, Shinmachi Nishihairu, Teranouchidori, Kamigyoku, Kyoto, Japan 7602; tel. 075-414-0808.) The price of Y4,000 ($30) per person includes breakfast.

In the moderate (for Japan) price range is the **Three Sisters Inn** (Inn Rakutoso Main, Okazaki, Sakyo-ku 606; tel. 075-761-6336). This charming traditional inn is owned by the Yamada sisters, who speak fluent English and take a personal interest in their guests, giving sightseeing tips and sometimes preparing special dinners for them. Located on a quiet street in the northwest section of the city, within walking distance of the Philosopher's Trail, it is an ideal place to stay for a sense of being in old Kyoto. It is an easy bus or cab ride from here to the central city. Rooms are furnished with tatami mats and futons. The lowest priced rooms have bathroom facilities down the hall; others have private baths. A traditional Japanese tub bath is available. If you stay at or near the Three Sisters Inn, you can begin your day in the proper meditative spirit by getting up early and walking to the end of Okazaki-dori and the Kurodani Temple, where you can watch the mist rise off the mountains as you listen to the monks chant and beat their drums. The price of Y7,800 ($60) for a single, Y15,600 ($120) double, includes continental breakfast. Also recommended is **Ryokan Murakamiya** (270 Sasya-cho, Shichijo-agaru, Higashinotouin-dori) just five minutes by foot from Kyoto Station. Japanese-style rooms with baths down the hall run about Y7,800 ($60) for two (tel. 075-371-1260; fax 075-371-7161). The staff is great, and English is spoken.

In the expensive category, the **Miyako Hotel** (Sanjo Keage, Higashiyma-ku, 605, tel. 075-771-7111) is a Western-style luxury hotel with a Japanese-style section. Located on a quiet hillside within easy walking distance of the Philosopher's Trail and Nanzenji, the Miyako has several restaurants as well as lovely gardens. Rooms start at Y19,000 ($144) for two.

Food

Kyoto cuisine is said to be milder, sweeter, and subtler than elsewhere, with emphasis on the flavor of fine ingredients rather than seasonings. One special place to try it is **Nakamura-ro** (Yasaka-jinja-uchi, Gion, Higashiyama-ku, open 11:30 a.m. to 7:30 p.m., last order 6:00 p.m.). Located next to the Yasaka Shrine, this restaurant is said to be the oldest in Japan and has been in the same family for 12 generations. Have tea and a snack at the ancient teahouse or an elegant *kaiseki* (Kyoto-style) dinner. A *bento* box lunch is also available from 11:30 a.m. to 3:00 p.m. Lunch costs from Y3,000 ($23), dinner from Y18,000 ($136).

Rokusei (71 Nishitenno-cho, Okazai, Sakyo-ku, open 11:30 a.m. to 8:00 p.m. except Monday when it is closed) is a special place for a fancy bento lunch, elegant tidbits served in shapely wooden buckets and lacquerware in a traditional setting. About Y2,800 ($21).

The above establishments are, let's face it, pricey. Many medium-priced restaurants display plastic models of their offerings in the window, clearly priced. This allows you to see (if not identify precisely) what you will get and also indicate to your waiter what you want to order. Bowls of rice with meat and vegetables or noodles with assorted toppings are often available, as well as such Western fare as pork cutlets and omelets.

There are many sushi bars in Kyoto. If you are a fan of these delicate rolls of rice and kelp with various morsels of raw fish or vegetables, ask about a place in the neighborhood of your hotel.

Other neighborhood options are the many *soba* (noodle) shops in town, where you can get a reasonably priced, tasty bowl of noodles in hot broth or, in summer, cool noodles with a special sauce—a Japanese-style pasta salad.

Several of the Buddhist temples have restaurants serving vegetarian fare in a quiet setting. One such is **Okutan** (86-30 Fukuchi-cho, open 10:30 a.m. to 6:00 p.m., seating until 5:30 p.m., Y3,000, or about $23), located on the grounds of the Nanzenji Temple.

The large *depaatos* (department stores) each have several restaurants with reasonably priced, easy to order, quickly served meals. In addition, department store basements are usually enormous markets with counters vending an assortment of prepared foods. It's fun to walk through and taste samples. Some items are sold at a discount just before closing time.

Most Western foods are called by their English names in Japanese. Just try pronouncing "orange juice" or "beefsteak" with a Japanese accent. The phrase "morning service" will get you coffee, white toast, and a soft-boiled egg at the local coffee shop, and "lunch set" designates a fixed-price lunch at some restaurants.

In a country where the price of sitting down in a restaurant for a cup of coffee or tea is legendary, it is good to know that vending machines dispensing beer and soft drinks can be found on nearly every street. Soft drinks usually cost Y100 ($.76).

Bus and Subway
Kyoto has an efficient bus and subway system. Bus fares are paid on exiting the front of the bus. Enter through the rear door and climb up the stairs immediately. If you remain on the stairs after the door closes, a buzzer will sound. A taped voice plays throughout the trip, announcing the stops in English as well as Kanji.

A one-day pass for unlimited use of the bus and subway can be purchased for Y1,050 ($8), Y530 ($4) for children under 12.

DAY 2
KYOTO: PHILOSOPHER'S TRAIL AND SHIJO STREET

One of Japan's most memorable walks, down the Philosopher's Trail, gives you a fine introduction to Zen Buddhism. In the afternoon, for contrast, you'll visit Shijo Street, Kyoto's busy, colorful shopping area.

Suggested Schedule

9:00 a.m.	Philosopher's Trail: Nanzenji Temple, Eikando Temple, Honen-in Temple, Ginkakuji Temple.
12:30 p.m.	Lunch.
1:30 p.m.	Shijo Street.
4:30 p.m.	Return by bus or taxi to your hotel.
5:00 p.m.	Afternoon tea and rest in your room.
6:00 p.m.	Dinner in your neighborhood. Early to bed.

Kyoto

Kyoto was the capital city of Japan for 1,000 years and is still considered its cultural capital, the heart of Japanese tradition. Well situated in a lovely valley surrounded by protective mountains, the city was laid out on a grid, modeled after a Chinese capital city, Chang-an. During World War II, the United States recognized the cultural importance of Kyoto and excluded it from the firebombings that destroyed Japan's other major cities. Kyoto is a densely populated city with approximately 1.5 million people in 610 square kilometers. There is an effort to preserve the historic old commercial and residential districts, although with land values five times those of Manhattan, zoning laws are understandably resisted by some. Nevertheless, many areas still feel peaceful and timeless, especially early in the morning before the cars awaken.

Kyoto can be hot and humid in summer and cold in winter. In spring, it is known for its cherry blossoms and in fall, for its blazing red maples.

If you are arriving in Japan from across the Pacific, jet lag will work in your favor because you will be waking up early. If you can remain awake until 8:00 p.m., you will sleep immediately and well. Rising at 4:00 a.m. is comparable to sleeping until noon in California. Kyoto, described by one resident as a "daytime city," is at its best in the early morning, when you can hear the monks chanting in the temples and watch the residents wash down their sidewalks, tend their streetside flowerpot gardens, or light a stick of incense at a corner shrine.

Visiting Kyoto for a short time immediately puts the tourist in a situation of high conflict. There is so much to see, much that requires slow, contemplative appreciation. How are you going to achieve that when your feet hurt or you are worried about getting to the next temple before it closes? (And Kyoto is said to have 1,000 temples!) Although we have included a lot to do here, our advice is: take your time, savor, and don't worry about missing something.

Zen Buddhism was imported from China in the twelfth century, and the headquarters of many of its major sects are in Kyoto. Many of the Japanese nobility deeded their summer palaces or retreats to Zen sects, which converted them into monasteries. Much care and expense went into the design of the buildings and gardens. Today we will visit a variety of these contemplative locales on the Philosopher's Trail. Temples are Buddhist; shrines are Shinto. Many Japanese are more or less observant of both—married at the shrine, buried at the temple.

It is a tradition for the pilgrim to carry a rice paper temple book, which you can purchase in a stationery store and mark with the elaborate red ink seals to be found at each temple. For this, a small contribution of Y200 to Y300 is expected. A temple book makes a lovely individualized souvenir.

Sightseeing Highlights

▲▲▲ **Philosopher's Trail**—From downtown or Kyoto Station, take the #5 bus to Nanzenji Temple. The quiet

Day 2

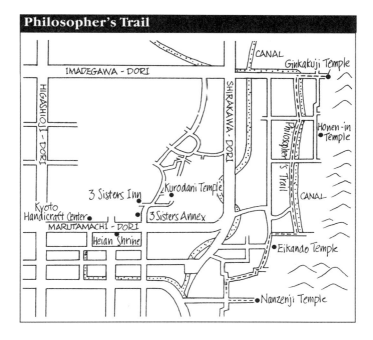

path known as the Philosopher's Trail, or Path of Philosophy, is a tranquil walk away from the bustle of the city. It follows a canal that runs along the foot of the eastern mountains, winding through a lovely, prosperous residential area and beginning and ending with renowned temples. You are never far from the sound of running water and sweeping brooms.

Begin at the southern end of the trail, with a visit to Nanzenji Temple. Situated in a pine forest, it was originally the palace of an emperor.

Next, proceeding north on the route, is Eikando Temple, which has a friendly, neighborhood feel to it. People stop here to worship in the early morning, and there is a nursery school on the grounds. Here, as in many of the temples, is a pond filled with a multicolored assortment of carp, dappled orange and black or buttery yellow.

You might want to stop across the street at the pleasant coffee shop frequented by taxi drivers. Then continue slowly up the shaded path, noting on both sides of the canal the substantial houses, many in the traditional Japanese style, others of subtle or opulent modern design. Here you will cross paths with the occasional dog walker or practitioner of t'ai chi ch'uan.

Soon you should begin looking carefully for the turn right to the Honen-in Temple. Match the characters on your map to those on the simple wooden marker. Ignoring the stairs that climb up the hill (they lead to a cemetery), turn left and continue on the road that parallels the canal path to the next broad flight of stairs that leads up the hill. Climb these and turn left, pausing at the gate to look down at the path to the temple, flanked by two rectangular mounds of raked sand with leaf patterns traced in them. (The patterns are changed according to the seasons.) Then follow the path over the bridge to the small temple and its empty, tranquil garden.

Continuing north, you will shortly leave this shaded calm for the approach to the Ginkakuji Temple, much visited by bus loads of uniformed schoolchildren (separate bus loads of boys and girls) and other pilgrims and tourists. This temple was built by a fifteenth-century shogun, Yoshimasa Ashikagu, as his villa and converted to a Zen temple after his death according to his will.

The Ginkakuji, or Silver Pavilion, is so named because the original plan, never carried out, was to cover it in silver leaf. The gardens surrounding it are especially notable for their sand shapes. One, named Ginshadan or "sea of silver sand," is modeled after a lake in China. The furrows on the sand represent the ripples in the water, on which the moonlight reflects, brightening the garden at night. Next to it is a small sand hill in the shape of Mt. Fuji. The shogun enjoyed watching the moon here.

By now you are probably hungry and ready for a glimpse of the central city. Take a cab or bus to Shijo Street to have lunch in one of the department stores and stroll through the shopping district.

▲▲ **Shijo Street**—Nowhere is the population density of Kyoto more apparent than in the downtown shopping district, jampacked with shoppers visiting elegant confectioners, antique stores, dress shops, and other establishments of all descriptions, a marked contrast to your morning of tranquillity and aesthetic satisfaction.

Stroll through the Daimaru Department Store, where you might see a young man demonstrating Shiseido cosmetics on a beautiful model and, on the third floor, young women eagerly examining the bright-colored dresses of fashionable Japanese designer Hanae Mori (only small women need apply).

In department store basements are extensive food markets. The bargain "basement" is on the top floor, where, in contrast to the usual restrained, tasteful displays, you will find a jumble of sale wares heaped on tables.

A block east of the Daimaru on the same side of the street, a large, handsome rectangular steel and enamel clock is suspended in front of a bank. On the odd-numbered hours during the day, its casing lifts to reveal a carousel of elaborate scenes—a treat for kids, who watch in suspense for the high-tech clock to strike and the colorful enamel figures to appear.

A block east of the Daimaru are the Teramachi and Shinkyogoku shopping arcades, where elegance rapidly gives way to glitz. North American shopping malls pale by comparison. If you are drawn by the unidentifiable mechanical noise, just for fun step into the huge Pachinko Omega and see row upon row of slot and pachinko (a form of gambling) machines, their avid players mesmerized by the loud music and the lure of the games in an atmosphere reminiscent of Las Vegas. A washbasin is thoughtfully provided at the exit; this is a country extremely conscious of cleanliness.

▲ **Gion**—From Shijo Street, it's an easy walk into the Gion district, center of Kyoto's nightlife. Walk east on Shijo Street, cross the river, and continue until you reach Hanamikoji-dori. Even if you are not tempted by this aspect of Kyoto, it is worth a stroll during the day for the understated architecture. You also might see a geisha or *maiko* (geisha's apprentice) hurrying along in her high clogs and elaborate kimono, face and shoulders painted white and hair elaborately dressed.

Helpful Hints

It is courteous and makes things go more smoothly to learn the basic expressions of politeness:

Good morning	oHIo gozaimasu
Good day	KoNIchiwa
Good evening	KonBANwa
Thank you	ArigaTO gozaimasu
Please	Kudasai

A few suffixes are helpful in getting oriented:

Street	-dori (e.g., Kawaramachi-dori)
River	-kawa/gawa (e.g., Katsurakawa)
Temple	-tera/dera (e.g., Kiyomizudera) or -ji (e.g., Ryoanji)
Shrine	Jinja/Jingu (e.g., Yasaka Jinja)

After a day or two you may find yourself bowing, or at least nodding your head in response to a bow, at the beginning and end of every conversational transaction—and sometimes in the middle, too.

People are uniformly courteous and helpful, although in the street they often look daunted and avert their eyes when approached by a lost foreign tourist with a map. Young students who might welcome a chance to practice their English are the best people from whom to seek help with directions.

Most tourists at the temples and palaces are Japanese, and therefore the tours are conducted in Japanese, but a small brochure is often provided in English, and English books are offered for sale.

The tourist information center, located on the first floor of the Kyoto Tower Building in front of Kyoto Station, is open from 9:00 a.m. to 5:00 p.m. on weekdays, 9:00 a.m. to noon on Saturdays. Telephone service is available from 9:00 a.m. to 5:00 p.m. daily throughout the year.

To visit the Imperial Palace and/or Shugakuin, you must apply in advance with your passport number to the

Day 2

Imperial Household Agency, located on the grounds of the Imperial Palace in the heart of the city. Phone (075) 211-1215 for details. Major tourist attractions are closed December 26 through January 5. The Imperial Palace, Shugakuin, and Katsura are also closed on Saturday afternoons and all day on the 2nd and 4th Saturdays and national holidays: December 25 to January 5, January 15, February 11, March 20 or 21 (depending on calendar Equinox Day), April 29, May 3 (Constitution Day), May 4, May 5 (Children's Day), September 15 (Old Age Day), September 23 and 24, October 10 (Health Sports Day), November 3, November 23 (Labor/Thanksgiving Day), and December 23.

It is a very good idea to get a bilingual map with both Japanese characters and the anglicized names for the major sightseeing attractions.

DAY 3
KYOTO: RYOANJI, KINKAKUJI, AND IMPERIAL PALACE

Spend your morning visiting two well-known temples in the northeast part of the city, Ryoanji and Kinkakuji. The excursion can be made comfortably in a morning, with plenty of time to return to the central city for the 2:00 p.m. tour of the Imperial Palace.

Remember that to visit the Imperial Palace, as well as the two Imperial villas, Shugakuin and Katsura, you must apply in advance with your passport number to the Imperial Household Agency (Day 2 "Helpful Hints"). This will surely be one of the most memorable tours on your itinerary.

Suggested Schedule

9:00 a.m.	Bus from Heian Shrine area to Kinkakuji (Gold Pavilion).
10:00 a.m.	Kinkakuji.
11:00 a.m.	Walk to Ryoanji.
11:30 a.m.	Ryoanji.
12:30 p.m.	Lunch at Yudofuya.
2:00 p.m.	Imperial Palace tour or Nijo Castle.
4:00 p.m.	Return to hotel by bus or taxi.
4:30 p.m.	Afternoon tea and rest.
5:30 p.m.	Dinner.
7:40 or 8:40 p.m.	Gion Corner.

Sightseeing Highlights

▲▲ **Kinkakuji (Gold Pavilion)**—Take the #205 bus from downtown or central station. This pavilion was built in 1395 by a shogun greatly influenced by the Chinese art of the Sung dynasty, and the Chinese style is most noticeable in the curled up pagoda corners of the top two roofs. The pavilion derived its name from the shogun's original plan, which was never carried out, to gild the third-story ceiling. In 1950, a disturbed monk burned down the original structure, and it was only when the replica was built that the exterior was gilded as it is seen today. The view of the structure across the pond and its reflection in the water are spectacular.

▲▲ **Ryoanji**—Walk down the hill from Kinkakuji (the two temples are off the same road) or take a short cab ride. This is the site of the best-known Japanese garden. A "dry" garden, it contains only stone and raked gravel, symbolizing water and landscape elements; bits of moss represent plantings. The rectangular plane contains fifteen stones carefully placed so that they can never all be seen from one vantage point.

The garden is enclosed on three sides by a low mud wall, terra-cotta in color, through which oil has seeped over the years to give the clay a subtle mottling that would be the envy of any potter. On the fourth side is a viewing platform, for the garden is not to be entered, only contemplated. Designed around 1500, it is a Zen garden intended for meditation; its spareness and abstract nature invite the significance the meditator brings to it.

However, this garden is a major tourist attraction. Here you are likely to be surrounded by uniformed schoolchildren counting the stones and blasted by a loudspeaker instructing about the place in Japanese. Perhaps a contemplative moment can be had here early in the morning or late in the afternoon; otherwise, enjoy the mostly Japanese visitors as part of the occasion.

▲▲ **Yudofuya**—If you continue past the dry garden down the path around the pond, you will come to a restaurant that will allow you a truly quiet, extraordinary experience. The restaurant, marked only by a small sign giving the menu, is entered through an exquisite small garden.

You will know you are nearing Yudofuya when you hear an irregular "tonk" of beaten hollow wood (you picture a monk with a drum). The sound is made by a stream flowing through one bamboo pipe down into another, carefully angled so that as it fills, the water causes it to tip and strike a rock.

The initial feel of the restaurant is quite austere and formal; it does not cater to foreign tourists but is not unwelcoming either. The menu is limited to tofu prepared in two or three ways. (When we asked at the entrance to the temple grounds where the restaurant was, the attendant responded, "Steak?" "No." "Bean restaurant?" "Yes.") You will be seated on cushions before small, round taborets facing out on the delicate garden and served a pot of tofu simmered with vegetables in a savory broth, with side dishes of colorful pickles. This must be the creamiest, most delicate tofu in the world, truly a meal to ease the heart and quiet the mind (if not the back) of the hard-working tourist.

▲▲▲ **Imperial Palace**—The Imperial Palace is located in the central city, on Marutamachi-dori. The #202 bus passes right by it. Kyoto was the site of the emperor's residence for 1,000 years, but this palace was only constructed in 1855, previous palaces having been destroyed by fire and warfare. Its grounds include 220 acres that serve as a tranquil central park for the city residents. Like most public and temple gardens in Kyoto, the grounds are carefully tended. Caretakers even pick up small fallen pinecones from the gravel with tongs.

An austere earthen wall capped with gray tile encloses the palace itself and 27 acres of grounds and gardens. Laden as most of us are with fairy-tale images of the castles of Europe, one may at first be unprepared for the dark woods and subtle sandy tones, the emphasis on gates and gardens, the simplicity of the rooms to be found here.

The guide will first lead you to the Emperor's Gate, constructed of many layers of cypress bark secured with bamboo nails. At one time, only the emperor was allowed to pass through the gate, although it is now occasionally used for guests on state visits. Beyond lies an enormous rectangular courtyard of raked sand, designed to reflect candlelight or moonlight.

Directly across from the gate is the Ceremonial Hall and, to its right, a Chinese-style building designed for the empress. Nine being a lucky number in Chinese tradition, eighteen signifies double happiness; therefore, the empress's pavilion is accessible by eighteen steps.

From the Ceremonial Hall, the guide (English-speaking here) will conduct you from building to building to view the various palace rooms through open sliding doors. Covered by thick tatami mats, most rooms are virtually empty of furniture, allowing the attention to focus on one ornament, such as an exquisite gold or silver screen.

Stand at one of the smaller gates leading from one section of the grounds to another and notice that from whatever angle you view the garden beyond, the gate frames an exquisite picture, perfectly balanced in light and shadow, shape and weight, and variety of texture—leaf and moss. All is Zen simplicity, a place designed for peace and meditation amid the affairs of state.

Tours are at 10:00 a.m. and 2:00 p.m. Monday through Friday and first and third Saturdays at 10:00 a.m. See Day 2 "Helpful Hints" for dates the palace is closed. Admission is free.

▲▲**Nijo Castle**—If you have not prearranged your visit to the Imperial Palace, this afternoon would be a good time to visit Nijo Castle, a short distance away. Built in 1603 by a shogun to serve as his Kyoto residence when he came from Edo (now Tokyo), it is surrounded by stone walls with turrets at two corners and consists of five profusely decorated buildings and a renowned garden. One still feels the shogun's presence in this fascinating castle. Open from 8:45 a.m. to 4:00 p.m. Closed December 26 to January 4. Admission is Y500 (about $3.80).

▲**Gion Corner**—For a sampling of traditional Japanese arts, attend a show at Gion Corner, where *bunraku* (classical puppetry), koto music, flower arranging, and the tea ceremony are displayed. Shows are at 7:40 p.m. and 8:40 p.m. and cost Y2,500 (about $19).

DAY 4
KYOTO: SHUGAKUIN, HEIAN SHRINE, AND KIYOMIZU TEMPLE

Arrange in advance with the Imperial Household Agency for permission to tour the imperial villa, Shugakuin, said to be the favorite of the Japanese. After a picnic or lunch near the Heian Shrine, you'll walk to the spectacular Kiyomizu Temple with time for last-minute shopping at the Kyoto Handicraft Center before dinner.

Suggested Schedule

10:00 a.m.	Shugakuin.
Noon	Lunch: Rosukei, near the Heian Shrine, or picnic at one of the nearby parks.
1:00 p.m.	Heian-Kiyomizu walk, including Heian Shrine, Choin-in, Yasaka Shrine, Kiyomizu Temple.
4:00 p.m.	Afternoon tea in hotel room.
5:00 p.m.	Kyoto Handicraft Center (15-minute walk from Heian Shrine) for last-minute shopping.
6:00 p.m.	Dinner in your neighborhood.
7:30 p.m.	Evening stroll.

Sightseeing Highlights
▲▲ **Shugakuin**—This imperial villa is located in the northeast part of the city, at the foot of Mount Hiei. Take the #5 bus from downtown, leaving about an hour before your scheduled tour time. Free fifty-minute tours are at 10:00 a.m. and 2:00 p.m. But you must apply, passport in hand, to join the tour at least 20 minutes before departure time. Visitors under 20 must be accompanied by an adult. Groups may not exceed nine persons per tour. The guided tours of the Kyoto Imperial Palace begin promptly; if you are late, you will be left behind and will have to reschedule at the Imperial Household Agency (tel. 075 211-1215). Give your destination to the bus driver; he will tell you where to get off. From the bus stop, the road to the villa

is clearly marked. It is a ten-minute walk gently sloping up through a pleasant residential neighborhood where incense burns at many street corner shrines. The villa, completed in 1659, consists of three teahouses built at staggered intervals up the mountainside.

The grounds here are vast and, probably because of their size, have a slightly less manicured look than some. This contributes to their charm. What is wonderful here is that much of the land is still under cultivation. Stretches of terraced rice paddies and vegetable gardens cover the slopes between the villas.

The teahouses themselves are simple and rustic, though beautifully designed. The focus is on the approach to them and the gardens and views, rather than on the buildings themselves. At one vantage point, from the middle villa, the view of the city disappears, leaving only the sight of the misty blue mountains and, directly below, a lovely lake with bridges. The long ascent to the uppermost villa is by a path cocooned in low pines. After the climb, you are rewarded by another perspective on the lake and distant mountains, complemented by a fresh view of the city below. This is a notable example of the Japanese landscape design technique of "borrowed scenery," incorporating a distant panorama into the overall garden picture. (See Day 2 "Helpful Hints" for dates the villas are closed.)

It is also possible to visit the Katsura Rikyu and Shugakuin Rikyu imperial villas as well as the Sento Gosho Imperial Palace. These locations can be visited only by permission of the Imperial Household Agency at Kyoto Gyoen-nai, Kamigyo-ku, Kyoto 602, Japan (tel. 075 211-1215). Write to them for the application form, enclosing a self-addressed envelope with International Postal Coupons. Visitors must be over 20 years of age and groups may not exceed four persons per tour.

▲▲▲ **Heian Shrine to Kiyomizu Temple**—Take an afternoon walk through the heart of the city and visit Kyoto's most beloved temples and shrines. From downtown or Kyoto Station, take the #5 bus to Heian Shrine.

These sites may be crowded with both visitors and

worshipers, especially on weekends. Begin at Heian Shrine and work your way up the hill to Kiyomizu Temple so you will not miss the dramatic approach to its lofty site. Pilgrims beware: the last part of the ascent is steep, so take it slow, especially if you are traveling in the heat of summer.

A relatively recent addition to the wonders of Kyoto, the Heian Shrine was constructed in 1895 to commemorate the eleven hundredth anniversary of Kyoto by honoring its founder, Emperor Kammu. The grounds are entered through a large, red lacquered gate. The buildings are laid out in a square around an immense gravel courtyard. Of chief appeal here are the lovely gardens that wrap around behind the buildings. They are entered on the west side of the courtyard (admission Y500, or about $4). The gardens have a modern, casual feel to them, with the focus on plant life rather than vistas. A large, oblong pond is traversed by a long, Chinese-style covered wooden bridge lined with benches where you can sit and feed the carp or eat a picnic lunch looking back toward the teahouse perched on one bank.

On Sundays this place is much visited by the Japanese. You will see many tour groups, each led by a guide with a flag, as well as families on outings and, on warm summer days, clusters of middle-aged women carrying parasols and fans. To the right of the gravel court as you enter the main gate, you may see a bride in her colorful kimono posing for a photo, as this seems to be a favorite place for weddings.

Marayuma Park is the principal public park of Kyoto. You might want to rest or picnic in its beautiful gardens between temple visits.

As you start the walk, Choin-in is located at the north gate of Marayuma Park. Erected in 1234 as a tribute to its founder, Honen, it is the headquarters of the Jodo sect of Zen Buddhism and a very active center of religious life. Its *hondo* (main hall), with its heavy wood and multiple gold hangings, is especially imposing.

As a break from temples and gardens, you might look

Day 4

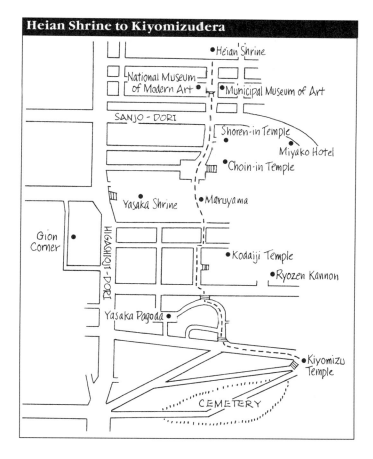

in at Yamanaka and Co., Ltd., located across from Shoren-in Temple, just up the street from Choin-in. This elegant and cordial shop presents the finest in modern ceramics and artwork, as well as a large room full of antique porcelain.

In sharp contrast to the massive construction of Choin-in is the poster-familiar spire of Yasaka Shrine, the five-storied pagoda with upturned Chinese-style roofs.

Kiyomizu Temple is the most beloved temple in Kyoto. It is located on Mt. Otowa, one of the city's eastern mountains. After ascending the narrow street, so raucous with souvenir and pottery shops that it is locally known as "teacup street," you arrive at the first pagoda and the imposing temple gate. The hondo, with its multilayered, cedar-thatched roof, is mounted on the hillside by an impressively heavy superstructure of exposed wooden crossbeams.

Stepping down on the eastern side of the main sanctuary, you come to the ancient waterfall known as Otowa No Taki, from which Kiyomizu, meaning "pure water," derives its name. A wooden cup with a long handle is provided so you can drink the water of the falls or pour it over your hands. Although you are aware of the bustling city below, the dark trees and sound of running water give a sense of being in a retreat deep in the mountains.

Originally founded in 780 and rebuilt in 1633, the temple is dedicated to Kannon Bosatsu, the incarnation of mercy and compassion. In front of the temple can be found a written appeal for world peace from the people of Hiroshima and Nagasaki.

▲**Kyoto Handicraft Center (Kumano Jinja Higashi, Sakyo-Ku)**—If you are a one-stop shopper, squeeze in a visit to this seven-story emporium of Japanese goods, from antique kimonos to transistors, located directly behind the gardens of the Heian Shrine. Several craftspeople can be seen at work: a potter, a wood-block artist, a weaver making an obi, or kimono sash. Here you can find incense, cotton and silk kimonos, fine porcelain, and pearls, as well as inexpensive coin purses and other souvenirs. Salespeople speak English. To get there, as you face the Heian Shrine looking north, turn left and walk to the first cross street (5 minutes). Turn right. Walk straight ahead to the first busy street (10 minutes). The handicraft center is slightly to your left on the north side of the street.

▲**Kawai Kanjiro's House (Gojo-zaka)**—For a pleasant change from shrines and temples, visit the home and kilns of Kawai Kanjiro (1890-1966), an influential potter, sculptor, writer, and leader in the revival of *mingei*, or

Japanese folk craft. His home, which he remodeled in the style of a rural cottage, is now open to the public with a display of his work. If you still have energy, consider this special place. From Kiyomizu Temple, descend the hill on foot and ask directions. The house is located in the warren of streets full of pottery shops at the base of the slope. (The nearest subway stop is Gojo. Ask for directions at the station.) Open 10:00 a.m. to 5:00 p.m. Closed Mondays and August 10 to August 20 and December 24 to January 7.

DAY 5
KYOTO TO BEIJING

Today's journey, three hours by air, is time travel at its finest. You will take off from high-tech Japan, where soft drink machine speakers persuade you to sip a beverage called Pocari Sweat, and land in an agrarian society where bicycles are the primary mode of transportation and the average per capita income is under $250. Entering the Middle Kingdom's capital, Beijing, you'll get a chance to go beyond the sightseeing routes of the organized tours to glimpse Chinese neighborhood life, and you'll have an opportunity to explore some of the many pleasures of shopping for arts and crafts along Wangfujing Street.

Suggested Schedule

7:00 a.m.	Depart Kyoto for Osaka.
10:50 a.m.	Depart Osaka for Beijing.
1:40 p.m.	Arrive in Beijing.
3:30 p.m.	Check into your hotel.

Afternoon and evening at leisure.

China

When asked his opinion of the French Revolution, Chairman Mao replied, "It's too early to say." Just about everyone in China has a long-term perspective, a fact that says a lot about some of the discoveries you'll make during the coming week. In a world where the emphasis is on instantaneous communication, the average Chinese citizen has no phone or television and receives less than a dozen letters a year. A 60-mile highway trip between the nation's second- and third-largest cities, Tianjin and Beijing, takes more than four hours. Although contemporary China is a desperately poor country, as it has been for 150 years, it has a rich cultural and mercantile legacy dating back to the twenty-first century B.C. One of the first nations to systematically embark on economic development, this enterprising society made pioneering efforts in agriculture, science, and technology. The Chinese were the first to smelt bronze, weave silk, and manufacture steel. Paper, printing, the compass, and gunpowder were all invented in China. As East Asian scholar Edward LeFevour puts it, "When Rome, Paris, and London were stinking medieval villages, China was the center of world trade. The Chinese, after all, were almost the inventors of capitalism."

But the same nation that could comfortably accommodate a population of 300 million is now pressed to the limit. In China, the simple logistics of feeding, housing, and educating more than 1.1 billion people consume much of the country's energy. Not surprisingly, a kind of industrial revolution mentality has set in, with little concern for environmental niceties. Nineteenth-century values are seen as a goal worth pursuing in a nation where millions of people still live in caves. While China abounds with world-class temples and gardens, memorable mountain parks, and, of course, superb arts and crafts, many urban centers are succumbing to utilitarianism. As those of us who live in the relative prosperity of America know, this kind of progress is a double-edged sword. Inevitably, cultural, artistic, and architectural traditions are sacrificed in the name of a more efficient society. Typical was the senseless decision to tear down portions of the historic wall surrounding Beijing's imperial center. The Cultural Revolution dealt another blow to some of the nation's finest antiquities. Fortunately, your visit comes at a time when the Chinese are becoming more protective of the landmarks that have made their nation so important in the history of civilization.

The visitor, of course, is the ultimate preservationist, eager to see the China of the Ming dynasty and the Empress Dowager. Although the number of visitors is growing rapidly, you are likely to find yourself treated with great respect by Chinese people eager to learn more about the West. You will be sought out by curious people who are eager to practice their English in a nation where the number of citizens studying our language exceeds the population of the United States.

Home to more than a fifth of the world's inhabitants, China remains, in many ways, one vast village square. Roughly 80 percent of the 1.1 billion Chinese live in the countryside, scattered among 275,000 villages. Even in the nation's largest cities, such as Beijing, village-style neighborhoods can be found in downtown areas.

Obviously, the populous Middle Kingdom is a busy place. Yet, even within China's largest metropolises, it's easy to find the sort of tranquillity one associates with Eastern religion and thought. Terraced gardens laced by waterfalls, towering pagodas, tranquil lakes, grand canals, and tree-lined boulevards add a graceful note to the Chinese cities you'll see. One of the world's safer tourist destinations, China has much to offer the visitor willing to venture beyond the official sightseeing route. If there is another country offering fine arts and crafts at more reasonable prices than China, we'd like to know about it. From the toy vendors on the street to the government gift shops selling fine silk goods, Chinese merchandise is an excellent value. There are certainly nations easier to visit than China. But as you will discover during your visit to Beijing, this nation remains an original in a world filled with cheap imitations.

Arrival

After claiming your luggage at the Beijing Airport, change your money at the Bank of China in the customs area. The official exchange rate is 5.3 yuan (Y) to $1. Keep in mind that the foreign exchange certificates (FEC) issued by the bank are the only currency major hotels and railways will accept from overseas tourists. Other establishments and cab drivers may ask for FEC because they are worth much more than *renminbi* (RMB), the regular Chinese currency known as People's Money. In addition, only FEC can be used to purchase certain luxury imports sold to foreigners in Friendship Stores but generally unavailable to the Chinese. Naturally, you will be offered a high exchange rate for FEC on the black market. While many nontourist establishments will accept RMB, foreigners are not allowed to exchange People's Money

Day 5   47

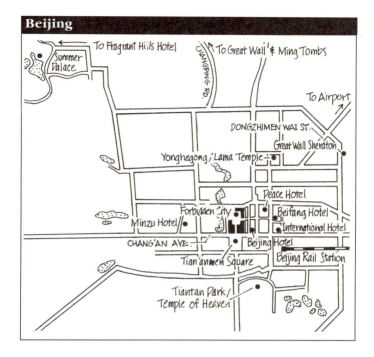

into dollars when they depart. Only FEC can be converted back into American currency.

A taxi to your hotel will run about Y100 ($20). Of course, you can reduce the fare by sharing the ride.

Lodging

A wave of new hotel construction in Beijing gives you many choices ranging from about Y230 to Y600 ($43-$162). Because your visit is a short one, consider a centrally located establishment such as the **Beijing Hotel**. While it is certainly not the most luxurious establishment in town, its location is unbeatable. Open to foreign visitors since 1979, the Beijing, alas, does not accept direct bookings from overseas tourists. Just ask your cab driver to take you to the hotel at 33 East Chang'an Avenue (tel. 513-7766). Even if you don't get your first choice, this complex with about 1,000 rooms is excellent,

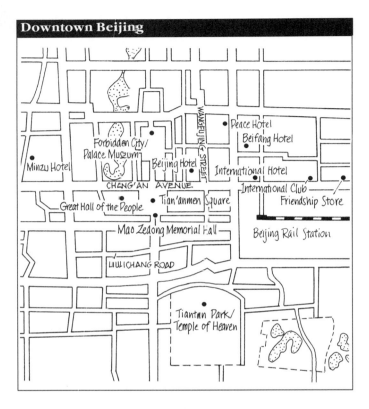

a short walk from Tian'anmen Square, adjacent to the shops of Wangfujing Street, night markets, and *hutongs* (alleyways) that will give you a feel for traditional Chinese neighborhood life. Room rates are a reasonable Y230 to Y315 ($43-$60). The ground floor offers one-stop shopping for gifts and tour packages, as well as a phone in the lobby with a direct connection to the United States. This hookup instantly links you to an American operator who will charge far less than the hotel switchboard for a call back home. Here you'll also be able to buy the English-language *China Daily*, an eight-page paper put out by an editorial staff of 600.

Another well-located hotel is the **Minzu Hotel** at 51 Fuxingmennei Avenue, just 2 miles west of Tian'anmen Square. Rooms here run about Y172 ($30). The restaurants and café are recommended (tel. 601-4466). Another convenient establishment is the **Beijing International Hotel** at 9 Jianguomenwai Dajie, across from the train station. This new hotel offers a good overview of the city, numerous restaurants, and convenient tour service. Rooms start at Y371 ($70) and can be reserved in advance (tel. 512-6688).

Located about 20 minutes east of Tian'anmen Square is the **Great Wall Sheraton** at 6A Donghuan Bei Road. Modeled after a Dallas establishment, it can be booked direct from home through Sheraton reservations. Rooms here run Y583 to Y901 ($110-$170). Phone 500-5566.

Food

You'll eat well at reasonably priced restaurants during your visit to China. Many of the best meals are found at the major hotels mentioned above. Among them is the **Beijing Hotel**, where the Szechuan restaurant is excellent. At the **Minzu Hotel**, food is first-rate at both the Western and Chinese restaurants. The **Fragrant Hills Hotel** (see Day 7) is a beautiful setting for tea or a snack. Recommended for lunch is the **Listening to the Orioles** restaurant at the Summer Palace (see Day 7). While prices for the dried fish in a sweet sauce and velvet chicken here are on the high side, the setting above Kunming Lake is memorable.

For Shandong food, such as braised shark fins and crisp chicken, try **Fengzeyuan**, 83 Xingfusancan (tel. 421-7508). The **Beijing Roast Duck Restaurant** on Dong San Huan Beilu, near the Zhao Long Hotel, is a good bet for that specialty. For vegetarian food, try **Beijing Sucai Canting** at 74 Xuanwumennei Street (tel. 654296). **Ritan Restaurant** in Ritan Park is a pleasant place to dine outdoors in good weather (tel. 592648).

Evening Ideas

Few moments in a traveler's life can equal the excitement of a first day in China. A friend of ours who teaches Chinese studies at an Oregon university vividly recalls the day fifteen years ago when she arrived in Beijing after a long train ride from Hong Kong. "When I got out of the train station, I was so excited I was literally screaming." Today, nearly every newcomer is quickly caught up in the excitement of this remarkable city, which is home to some of the world's most famous monuments, palaces, and shrines. Every aspect of the lives of the Chinese, from childbirth to cemetery plots, is affected by decisions of the Communist party headquarters here.

A good place to begin your visit is Beijing's shopping hub, Wangfujing Street. Start on the east side of the Beijing Hotel and work your way north past the department stores, where you can shop for silk, embroidery, and arts and crafts at remarkable prices. For many of the older Chinese, picking out new clothes is an easy matter. To them, the fall and spring lines are one and the same, drab blue or gray uniforms that give racks the look of a wardrobe department for a Civil War movie. But you'll also find hipper styles set out for the young and young at heart. As you might expect in a nation that produces heavily for the American market, many of these garments look like the kind of thing you might find in Chicago or Los Angeles.

Turn down one of the back lane *hutongs* at the dinner hour and you'll get a quick introduction to family life Chinese style. Here, Beijing residents are packed into courtyard housing that was the cornerstone of the Chinese community for centuries. Known as *siheyuan*, these simple brick-walled houses often grew to accommodate several generations under one roof. Wealthy men added extra rooms or even entire compounds to accommodate second or third wives, in-laws, and servants. After the revolution, many of these relatively large units were divided into housing for several families and rented out by the government at a few dollars a month. Every room seems to serve a double or, in some cases, a triple purpose. One family per room seems to be the rule of thumb, with the living room almost always doubling as sleeping quarters.

In the hutongs off Wangfujing Street (north of the Beijing Hotel), you'll see husbands biking down the street with a son on the handlebars and wife on the back fender. You may also spot young couples embracing in public view, a scene unthinkable not long ago in tradition-bound China. There may even be workmen scooping up wet garbage from the neighborhood slop pile to fertilize a nearby garden the following day.

   Continue north on Wangfujing Street and you'll run into a night market, where entrepreneurial Chinese are encouraged to dabble in capitalism. When you've finished exploring, head back to the Beijing Hotel for a drink and a chance to compare notes with fellow guests who shared your good sense and chose this remarkable destination.

DAY 6
BEIJING: THE GREAT WALL AND TIAN'ANMEN SQUARE

Today you'll visit the only man-made structure visible from outer space, the Great Wall. After climbing this landmark, visit the Ming Tombs and then return to Beijing to walk through vast Tian'anmen Square, where the People's Republic began.

Suggested Schedule

7:00 a.m.	Breakfast at your hotel.
8:00 a.m.	Leave for the Great Wall.
9:30 a.m.	Climb the Great Wall.
1:00 p.m.	Ming Tombs.
4:00 p.m.	Tian'anmen Square.
Evening	Explore the city, shop, attend an acrobat show, puppet theater, or opera.

Travel Route

Today's itinerary is a 70-mile loop north of Beijing. For about Y200 ($37), you and up to three companions can hire a taxi at your hotel (hotels are usually the easiest places to catch cabs in China) for the day's outing to the Great Wall, the Ming Tombs, and back to Tian'anmen Square. This approach will, of course, make it easy to go at your own pace. Alternatively, join one of the tours to the Great Wall and the Ming Tombs leaving from the Qiao Yuan Hotel about 9:00 a.m.

Sightseeing Highlights

▲▲▲ **The Great Wall**—The walls that surround the traditional Chinese home provide a measure of seclusion for many residents of this crowded country. But the nation's most famous wall has long since outlived its usefulness. Begun in small sections during the fifth century B.C., the wall was linked up two centuries later in a massive ten-year effort during the Qin dynasty. It took 180

Day 6

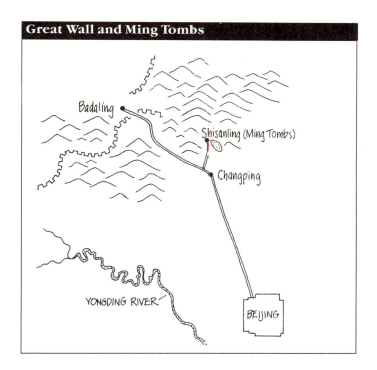

Great Wall and Ming Tombs

million cubic meters of compressed earth, enough to create a road that could circle the globe three times, to complete this 3,800-mile-long fortification. Besides protecting the nation, the Great Wall was a vital communication link across northern China. While much of the wall is now in ruins, the section you will visit today at Badaling (Eight Prominent Peaks) has been meticulously restored.

A remarkable piece of engineering, the wall doesn't just cross the Middle Kingdom; it winds through the countryside, ascending mountains and plunging down into remote valleys. Sturdy walking shoes are essential for today's climb. Visitors who are physically limited will not be able to ascend the wall. Although the hike to the right is less strenuous, tourists in good physical condition should consider making the trip up the left side. This steep climb leads to a beacon tower that was used to send messages by smoke, fire, and, later, gunfire signals. This system could transmit a communiqué over 300 miles in a few hours. Today, the tower at Badaling is an excellent vantage point for photos of the wall and this strategic pass. After making your descent, pass under the wall into Badaling village. Amid the souvenir stands, you will find exhibits of arts and crafts and possibly a special museum show. For example, in 1988 one traveling exhibit featured many of the famous terra-cotta army soldiers from the tomb of Emperor Qin Shihuang at Xian. Keep an eye out for similar finds during your visit.

▲▲ **Ming Tombs**—The Great Wall section you've just seen dates back to the Ming dynasty. About an hour from the wall, the Ming necropolis is the final resting place for 13 of the 16 Ming emperors. Construction began in 1409 and ended in 1644 with a tomb built for the last Ming emperor by the first Qing emperor. The tombs themselves are something of a letdown, crowded and filled with second-rate replicas. More impressive is the Sacred Way leading up to the tombs. After passing under an arched marble gate, you'll come to the legendary Avenue of the Animals. A highlight of any trip to China, it features 24 giant stone animals and a dozen stone human figures carved in the fourteenth century. After the Ming line ended, a Qing emperor tried to move this rock-ribbed honor guard to his own burial place. The idea was dropped after the emperor was warned that any relocation would bring down an eternal curse from the Ming Tombs.

▲▲ **Tian'anmen Square**—The birthplace of the People's Republic in October 1949, this 100-acre square is named for Tian'anmen Gate, built in the seventeenth century. It was here that the emperor's edicts were lowered to waiting ministers in the mouth of a carved golden phoenix. In June 1989, Chinese troops massacred hundreds of pro-democracy demonstrators and injured thousands more in a horrifying assault. It was one of the darkest moments in late twentieth-century Chinese history. Perhaps the best-known building here is Mao's

Tomb, located within sight of a Kentucky Fried Chicken outlet (foreigners must line up separately from locals and pay four times as much for the identical finger-lickin'-good bucket). To see Mao in repose, you must first check all your belongings and then join the long line for a brief glimpse of China's famous revolutionary, who took power in 1949. The sheer scale of Tian'anmen Square makes it a great vantage point for viewing city life. To the south of the square is the Great Hall of the People, China's most important political forum. In addition to a 10,000-room assembly hall, there are meeting rooms for all 30 provinces, each furnished with local handicrafts. On the east side of the square are the Museum of the Chinese Revolution and the Museum of Chinese History.

Nightlife
After leaving the square, you may want to return to Wangfujing Street to browse or head over to Liulichang Street to shop for antiques. A good place to find Han ceramic reproductions, vases, and rubbings of ancient stone carvings is **Jiguge**. It's located at 136 East Liulichang Street (tel. 335698). Recommended evening activities include enjoying a Peking duck dinner and watching acrobats at the Dazhalan Acrobatics Theater or the Beijing Gymnasium. Also popular are the China Puppet Drama Troupe and the city's four opera companies. An opera house convenient to the Beijing Hotel is the **Capital Theater** on Wangfujing Street (tel. 554877).

DAY 7
BEIJING: THE FORBIDDEN CITY

Round out your first week in Asia by visiting three of the region's greatest treasures: the Forbidden City, the Temple of Heaven, and the Summer Palace.

Suggested Schedule

8:00 a.m.	Breakfast at your hotel.
9:00 a.m.	Visit the Forbidden City.
Noon	See the Temple of Heaven.
1:30 p.m.	Lunch at Listening to the Orioles restaurant, Summer Palace.
4:30 p.m.	Depart Summer Palace for your hotel. Evening at leisure.

Travel Route
The easiest way to reach today's highlights in Beijing is by taxi. If you want to avoid the necessity of hailing a cab after visiting each site, you can book a driver for the entire day. Tour companies leaving from major Beijing hotels cover today's highlights. Just be sure they allow adequate time at each destination.

Sightseeing Highlights
▲▲▲ **The Forbidden City** —What can you say about a 9,000-room palace that was home to 24 Ming and Qing emperors and later was featured in a Bertolucci movie? Plenty, if you're not struck dumb by the most remarkable imperial palace this side of Versailles. Easily reached by taxi, the Forbidden City is one of Beijing's most visited sights. Accordingly, the Chinese government plans to curtail the number of visitors allowed on busy days. Avoid disappointment by arriving early to make the most of this opportunity to visit the vast complex that was both the private and administrative headquarters of the emperor. Construction of the palace, which is protected by high walls, a moat and a watchtower, was started in the thirteenth century and was completed about 1420.

The imperial family lived here along with thousands of concubines, eunuchs, ministers, artisans, and other personnel. Although much of the palace's finest art was stolen by Chiang Kai-shek's forces before they fled to Taiwan, the Palace Museum remains one of China's best.

At times the Forbidden City seems like a kind of royal maze, with gates opening onto courtyards leading to palace halls where you step out onto terraces that lead to yet other gates and courtyards. Seemingly endless, the city spreads out along three parallel walkways. Begin your tour on the central path and then explore the buildings along the parallel north and south walkways. Among the highlights you'll see along the way are the Hall of Supreme Harmony, the Hall of Preserving Harmony, and the Golden Throne Hall. The largest building in the Forbidden City, the Hall of Supreme Harmony has 40 gilded doors. The emperor made his way up the marble steps to his golden throne the easy way. He was carried in a litter. Other landmarks include the carved stone ramp behind the Hall of Preserving Harmony and the remarkable throne room in the Hall of Mental Cultivation. The Forbidden City is open from 8:30 a.m. to 5:00 p.m. Ticket sales end at 4:30 p.m.

▲▲ **Temple of Heaven**—For almost five centuries, Chinese emperors came to this complex, one of China's largest group of temple buildings, to pray for a bountiful harvest. Easily reached today by taxi from the Forbidden City, the three temple buildings are located in one of the city's biggest parks.

Begun in 1420, the Temple of Heaven took fourteen years to complete. The three temple buildings are enclosed by a northern circular wall representing heaven and a southern wall that stands for earth. The Hall of Prayer for Good Harvests, rebuilt after it was torched by a lightning strike in 1889, is considered one of the great achievements in Chinese architecture. No nails were used to create this 114-foot-high wooden structure topped by a triple-cone blue tile roof. The smaller Imperial Vault of Heaven is surrounded by the Echo Wall, where whisper-

Summer Palace and Fragrant Hills

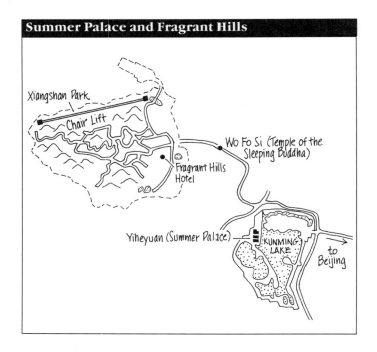

ing can easily be heard by a listener standing at an opposite point on the wall. Open 6:30 a.m. to 6:00 p.m.

▲▲▲ **The Summer Palace**—To escape the summer heat, the imperial family retreated to this 700-acre getaway on the northwest side. Take a taxi to this twelfth-century palace. It was sacked by French and English troops in 1860, rebuilt in 1888 by Empress Dowager Cixi, destroyed again by invaders in 1900, then rebuilt a second time by the dowager in 1903. Hans Christian Andersen and the entire Disney organization couldn't have created a better fairy-tale setting than this lakeside park with its ten-story temple, formal gardens, and pavilions.

Eager to protect themselves from the elements, Chinese rulers built a 2,100-foot-long covered gallery running from the Gate Inviting the Moon to the Pavilion of Stone Inscriptions. According to the book *Magnificent China*, this path is so long that Beijing locals say a couple could utter their first words of love at the beginning of the walkway and set their wedding date at the end. Some tours try to rush you through the palace. That's a mistake, particularly in spring when the lotus trees blossom. Allow several hours to enjoy the Imperial Gardens, Kunming Lakefront, Longevity Hill, and the Sea of Wisdom Tower. If you wish, lunch at Listening to the Orioles restaurant.

The Summer Palace is open 7:00 a.m. to 6:00 p.m. Afterward, you may, if time permits, taxi to the Temple of the Sleeping Buddha and Fragrant Hills Park. Also known as Western Hills Park, this is an excellent area to hike if you have an extra day in Beijing. The Fragrant Hills Hotel is one of the city's architectural landmarks and a good place to stop for tea or a snack.

DAY 8
BEIJING TO SHANGHAI

After visiting one of Beijing's most impressive temples, depart the Chinese capital to visit the nation's largest metropolis, Shanghai, home to 13 million people. As you'll see today, it is also an irresistible time warp for connoisseurs of the recent past.

Suggested Schedule

8:00 a.m.	Breakfast at your hotel.
9:30 a.m.	Visit Yonghegong (Lama) Temple.
11:00 a.m.	Return to your hotel.
Noon	Depart Beijing.
Afternoon	Fly to Shanghai.
Evening	Jazz at the Peace Hotel.

Sightseeing Highlight

▲▲ **Yonghegong (Lama) Temple**—Located in the city's eastern district, this lamasery is the home of a Buddhist sect incorporating both Hindu and Tibetan religious worship. Lamaism was promoted by the Qianlong emperor to maintain harmony with both Mongolia and Tibet. Built in 1694 and still managed by Lamaist monks, red-walled Yonghegong is one of the city's most prized temples. While it is much smaller than other landmarks you have visited in Beijing, Yonghegong is a gem that survived wholesale destruction during the Cultural Revolution, thanks to the intervention of Zhou Enlai. Among the highlights are the Buddhas of the Three Ages in the Yonghedian Hall. The gardens are some of the city's best. Open 8:00 a.m. to 5:00 p.m.; ticket sales end at 4:00 p.m. Closed Tuesdays and Thursdays.

Flight to Shanghai

Be sure to book your taxi at the hotel desk at least an hour before departure time. Allow extra time for delays at the airport. Leave downtown Beijing 2 hours before flight time. On arrival in Shanghai, take a taxi to your hotel.

Shanghai

Time appears to have stood still in this faded capital that seems to have more in common with the capitals of northern Europe than those of Asia. The mansions are Tudor and classical French in style, hotels have an art deco look, and office blocks are Gothic, neoclassical, and baroque. Clearly, this is one of the world's great urban set pieces. Except for a handful of modern high-rises erected in the past few years, Shanghai looks very much like the Asian financial capital it was during the first half of this century. Unlike other major cities in this part of the world, including several in China, Old Shanghai has not turned against its past by sacking historic districts to erect vast numbers of apartment complexes. Today, about half of Shanghai's 13 million residents live in what is loosely referred to as Old Shanghai. This is only a small portion of the 2,355-square-mile greater Shanghai district, a vast urban and rural region. Fortunately, it is a preservationist's dream, a city that has just said no to the wrecker's ball, the highway developer's cloverleaf, and the blights of redevelopment and urban removal.

Although the wealthy expatriate community is a distant memory, you can still see their mansions, which have been turned into children's palaces, enrichment centers that cater to the city's best and brightest young people. Many of the lavish apartment blocks are still here, serving today as housing for the proletariat.

Call it a historical accident, benign neglect, or, if you prefer, a Communist plot. In any case, Shanghai is a museum without walls, a city where it is possible to easily find the touchstones of the Chinese revolution, the home of Sun Yat-sen, and the theater where a starlet named Jiang Qing tried to launch her career. (Later, she would end up marrying a young man named Mao Zedong.)

A city where anything was possible, prerevolutionary Shanghai was home to millionaires who put blankets over the engines of their limousines during the winter months, while the poor died of exposure by the thousands in the streets. Here, gangster Du Yueshang one-upped Al Capone by sending a casket instead of flowers to an enemy's home. The city's image was popularized in numerous books and films like *Shanghai Express*, in which Marlene Dietrich boasted, "It took more than one man to change my name to Shanghai Lily." Even the missionaries had never seen anything like it. According to Pan Ling, author of *In Search of Old Shanghai*, they "declared that if God let Shanghai endure he owed an apology to Sodom and Gomorrah."

Under these circumstances, it is no surprise that the Chinese Communists got their start here. "No other city fell to communism in so feverish a whirl of pleasure, dissoluteness, rapacity, and squalor," says Pan Ling. While the capitalists were sent packing, the prostitutes and opium addicts were rehabilitated for more respectable professions, the worst slums were cleaned up, and child labor was eliminated. Drug peddlers who didn't give up their old ways were executed. In this way, Shanghai became transformed. While the city is certainly not part of the affluent society, it remains one of the most cosmopolitan spots in China and, of course, one of the most popular destinations in Asia.

Lodging

For location, ambience, and a sense of history, it's hard to beat the **Peace Hotel**, originally known as the Cathay. Situated on Nanjing Road, at the Bund, it was built by entrepreneur Victor Sassoon, who made a killing in the opium trade. Among the distinguished guests who favored the Cathay was Noel Coward, who finished up *Private Lives* at this 14-story landmark. The hotel is divided into two buildings; foreign visitors usually choose the northern wing (getting a room in the southern wing is difficult). Rooms run from Y140 to Y400 ($26-$76). Equipped with modern business facilities and a China International Travel Service (CITS) desk, this is a convenient place to stay. While the Peace Hotel certainly could use some spiffing up, the wonderful jazz band and popular eighth-floor dining room make it our first choice in Shanghai. The northern wing is located at 20 Nanjing Road. Tel. 321-1244.

# Day 8

Another popular hotel convenient to central Shanghai is the vast **Jinjiang** at 59 Maoming Road, with rooms ranging from neo-Charlie Chan to motel modern. Originally built as a group of apartment blocks, the 700-room Jinjiang comes complete with a bowling alley, billiard room, and supermarket. Rooms at this European oasis start around Y150 to Y300 ($28-$57). Tel. 258-2582. Another excellent possibility is the **Hua Ting Sheraton** at 1200 Cao Xi Bei Lu Road. About halfway between the riverfront and the airport, this 1,000-room high-rise is one of the most modern in town. Make reservations through Sheraton. Rooms start around $94. Tel. 386000. The **Jing'an Guest House** at 370 Huashan Lu is another good choice, with rates starting around Y160 ($30). The rooms are fine, and there's a first-class bakery on the premises. Tel. 255-1888.

Food

The Peace Hotel's **Dragon and Phoenix Restaurant** offers a variety of Shanghai, Szechuan, and Cantonese dishes, as well as Western cuisine. From the eighth floor there is also a fine view of the Bund. The **Old Shanghai Restaurant** (see Day 9) in the Yuyuan Bazaar is another good bet for Shanghai dishes. It's located at 242 Fuyou Lu (tel. 282782). The **Dongfeng Hotel** restaurant at 3 Zhongshang Dong is the former Shanghai Club and home of the famous long bar (see Day 9). The Park Hotel's **Four Seasons Banquet Room** is a good choice for Peking duck. Order in advance by calling 327-5225 (see Day 11). Another good possibility for Szechuan food is the **Meilongzhen Jiujia** at 22 Nanjing Street, 1081 Long Lane (tel. 256-2718). Specialties include crisp-fried duck and imperial chicken. **Renmin (People's) Restaurant** at 226 Nanjing Road (tel. 320-1763) is recommended for its Shanghai dishes. The eighth-floor dining room at the **Jing'an Guest House,** 370 Huashan Road (tel. 255-1888), serves good Szechuan dishes. Also try **Southland** at 813 Beijing Road East (tel. 220480). It's near the Park Hotel.

Evening
After dining at the Peace Hotel's eighth-floor restaurant, head down to the coffee shop to hear the jazz band, formed in the late 1940s and directed by Zhou Won Rong. Zhou and his colleagues, Chou Te Ping on piano, Gu Gin Long on tenor sax, Wong Jin Ming on alto, Zhou Hong Bin on bass, and Chen Yu Chang on drums, were all rising stars on the Chinese jazz scene; but in 1953, a few years after the revolution, the government suggested that it was time for this jazz group to take a break. The break lasted for 27 years. Only in 1980, after the death of Mao and the end of the Cultural Revolution, did the Communist party finally decide the time was right for Western jazz to return to Shanghai. After nearly three decades of working classical venues like the Shanghai Symphony Orchestra, the group resumed jamming. "We just picked up right where we were before the revolution," says jazz band leader Zhou.

Patrons returning to the Peace Hotel after a long hiatus did a double take as they found the musicians, now in their 60s and 70s, packing the house with tunes like "Harbor Lights" and "In the Mood." Ask them to play some of your favorite oldies, and they'll probably oblige.

DAY 9
SHANGHAI: THE BUND, YUYUAN GARDEN, AND SHANGHAI MUSEUM

Today you'll explore the Bund, once the hub of colonial power in Asia. After a walk through the Yuyuan Garden and a visit to the vast Yuyuan Bazaar, move on to the city's finest museum. The evening is reserved for Shanghai's world-famous acrobats.

Suggested Schedule

8:00 a.m.	Breakfast at your hotel.
9:00 a.m.	Stroll the Bund.
10:30 a.m.	Visit Yuyuan Garden and Wuxingting Teahouse.
12:30 p.m.	Lunch at the Old Shanghai Restaurant.
2:00 p.m.	Visit the Shanghai Museum of Art and History.
Evening	Attend the Shanghai Acrobatic Theater.

Travel Route

From your hotel, head to Huangpu Park, across from the Peace Hotel. Walk south along the Bund (Zhongshan Road) and turn right on Fuyou Road to the Yuyuan Garden (or, if you prefer, catch a taxi). The Wuxingting Teahouse is located in the Yuyuan Bazaar area adjacent to the garden. Also here is the Old Shanghai Restaurant at 242 Fuyou Lu (tel. 282782). From here, walk north on Henan Road to the Shanghai Museum of Art and History (adjacent to the intersection of Yan'an Road).

To see the Shanghai Acrobatic Theater, catch a taxi to the dome at 400 Nanjing Road.

Hint: you'll want to book tomorrow's train ticket for Suzhou today at the Peace Hotel CITS desk. Try for one of the early trips. Alternatively, you can purchase your ticket at the train station's foreign passenger ticket office. It's easily reached by cab.

Sightseeing Highlights

▲▲▲ **The Bund**—Until the mid-nineteenth century, Shanghai was a small port and silk trading center. Only after 1842, when China was defeated by the British during the Opium War, did business begin flourishing along an obscure Huangpu riverfront towpath known as the Bund. With the city now open to foreign investors, Westerners began turning Shanghai into a Middle Kingdom boomtown. To lure them, "international concessions" were created for the British, French, Americans, and eventually the Japanese. Within these regions, foreigners were exempt from Chinese law. This was heaven for overseas entrepreneurs, who paid a lower tax rate than natives hired for a pittance to work twelve-hour shifts. By the end of the century, Shanghai became a city of one million and a major global trading center. The Bund, now called Zongshan Road, became home base for the great trading companies, banks, customs houses, shipping lines, hotels, and private clubs that stood at the heart of this foreign trade center.

One of the busiest waterfronts in Asia, the Bund docks are reached via the 60-mile-long Huangpu Channel from the Yellow Sea. As a security precaution, the Chinese refuse to publish the tide charts, which are critical for safe passage over the shallow sandbars found along the route. In addition, the channel markers are regularly shifted to protect against foreign invaders. Non-Chinese ships bound upriver are given the correct channel route by a harbor pilot just a few hours before reaching the Huangpu.

If you rise early in the morning and walk over from the Peace Hotel to Huangpu Park, you'll find hundreds of Chinese doing their morning t'ai chi ch'uan. In colonial times, these public gardens were reserved for the British. Signs prohibited entry by dogs or Chinese unless they happened to be hired help assisting their employers. As you walk along the Bund, you could swear someone has turned back the clock 40 or 50 years. Although the Customs Building clock tower no longer chimes the Cultural Revolution anthem, "The East is Red," this remains a good place to catch the rhythm of Shanghai. While conspicuous consumption is clearly out in a city where the average income is about $235 a year, contemporary Shanghai still has its French bakeries and trendy shops that set the pace for Chinese fashion. Antique auto buffs will be intrigued by the ubiquitous Shanghai car, a widely seen Packard-like vehicle that is a Chinese classic. On the Bund you can also see many of the European-style buildings that were the hub of the former capitalist economy, such as Jardine Matheson and the Hong Kong and Shanghai Bank. Inside the Dongfeng Hotel at 3 Zhongshan Road is the famous long bar that was a mandatory stop on any pre-1949 visit to Shanghai. It was the heart of a male bastion called the Shanghai Club. Today, this famous landmark is a restaurant where guests are served Shanghai cuisine on the 100-foot-long mahogany bar.

▲▲ **Yuyuan Garden**—This sixteenth-century garden is a preview of tomorrow's trip to Suzhou. Built for the Ming dynasty, this is the city's best-known Chinese garden. More than 30 beautiful pavilions, lotus ponds, teahouses, and a 400-year-old ginkgo tree make this a fine refuge from the busy city. Sculptured stone dragons lie in wait on top of every wall. To keep you oriented, every spot in the garden is identified with a name like "Pavilion for Viewing Frolicking Fish" or "Corridor for Approaching the Best Scenery." The garden, open for admission from 8:00 a.m. to 10:30 a.m. and 2:00 p.m. to 5:00 p.m. (visitors inside before 10:30 a.m. may stay), is adjacent to the Yuyuan shopping district. You'll have plenty of choices at the hundreds of stalls here which offer over 16,000 items, including all kinds of arts and crafts. Specialty shops in this part of town focus on everything from snuff to walking sticks. Prices are particularly good on small items, such as children's puppets. The five-sided Wuxingting Teahouse is a picturesque spot for a break.

▲▲ **Shanghai Museum of Art and History**—After lunch, walk to this museum to see its outstanding collection covering 5,000 years of Chinese history. At the museum you'll find bronzes from the Xia, Shang, and Zhou dynasties. Also here are neolithic ceramics, ancient vases, figures from Xian's terra-cotta army, cloisonné, lacquerware, embroidery, and paintings from the Tang and Song periods. Don't miss the museum gift shop, where you can find beautiful landscape paintings, lacquerware, cloisonné, embroidery, and colorful hand-painted notecards. Each purchase is beautifully wrapped in a brocade box. The reasonable prices make this an excellent place to shop for gifts. The museum is open 9:30 a.m. to 11:30 a.m. and 1:30 p.m. to 5:00 p.m. During the rest of the afternoon you may want to explore this great city on foot. You can pick up tickets for the Shanghai Acrobatic Theater at 400 Nanjing Road (tel. 564051). Performances are staged daily except Tuesdays.

DAY 10
SUZHOU

An hour-long train ride takes you west to Suzhou, the Grand Canal town with a green thumb. You'll have an entire day to see some of China's finest landscape architecture at the city's meticulously restored gardens.

Suggested Schedule

5:30 a.m.	Breakfast at your hotel.
6:50 a.m.	Catch the morning train to Suzhou.
8:00 a.m.	Arrive in Suzhou.
8:30 a.m.	North Temple Pagoda.
9:30 a.m.	Suzhou Museum.
10:30 a.m.	Humble Administrator's Garden.
Noon	Lunch at Suzhou Hotel.
1:00 p.m.	Garden of the Master of Nets.
2:00 p.m.	Surging Wave Pavilion.
3:00 p.m.	Garden of Harmony.
4:00 p.m.	Return to the station and catch the train to Shanghai.

Travel Route

If you did not purchase an advance ticket for the Suzhou train as recommended on Day 9, it's a good idea to arrive early at the Shanghai train station foreign booking office. Service is frequent, but these trains are heavily booked and schedules are subject to change. After arriving in Suzhou, head for the foreign booking office to purchase your return ticket (train tickets are sold one-way). The Y12 ($2.28) train trip takes about an hour and ten minutes. In Suzhou, you can take cabs to the temples and museums or, if you're feeling ambitious, rent a bike for Y10 ($1.90) across from the train station. Head south on Renmin Road to the North Temple Pagoda Then turn left (east) down Taohuaqiao Road. Shortly after the street name changes to Beisita Road, you'll reach the Suzhou Museum. Next door is the Humble Administrator's Garden. Then return west on Beisita Road to Lindun Road and turn left (south). At Ganjiang Road, turn left and continue south on Fenghuang Road. Turn left (east) on Shiquan Street to the Suzhou Hotel. Then return west on Shiquan Street to the Master of Nets Garden. Continue west on Shiquan Street to Renmin Road and turn left (south) to the Surging Wave Pavilion. Return north on Renmin Road to Ganjiang Road and turn left to the Garden of Harmony. Continue north on Renmin Road to the train station. Total biking distance is about ten miles.

Sightseeing Highlights

Founded in the fifth century B.C., Suzhou flourished with the construction of the Grand Canal, completed in A.D. 618. Thanks to its strategic location on the world's longest man-made waterway, the city became a major shipping center. While Suzhou lacks the majesty of Venice, it's an inviting city with graceful bridges and artisans who offer visitors some of the country's finest silk and embroidery. On weekends, large crowds, primarily visitors from other Chinese communities, visit this city of 670,000. Suzhou's leading attractions are its gardens, built several centuries ago by the city's gentry, many of them silk merchants. Of the more than 100 major gardens, ten are fully restored and welcome visitors. Walled off from the surrounding city, these sanctuaries are considered a national treasure.

▲**North Temple Pagoda**—Climb this nine-story temple and you'll get a good overview of the garden city. Behind this seventeenth-century landmark you'll find a popular teahouse.

▲▲**Suzhou Museum**—Before visiting your first garden, stop here to learn about some of the artistic traditions of this city that grew rich on silkworms; there are impressive silk and embroidery exhibits. The exhibits also provide an introduction to the city's political and cultural history. This is a good place to learn about the Grand Canal's crucial role in Chinese economic development.

▲▲▲**Humble Administrator's Garden**—A Suzhou favorite, where eager lines of visitors make their way

Day 10

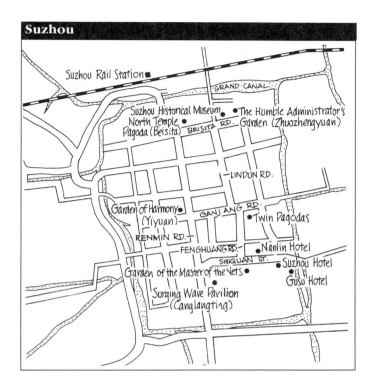

Suzhou

along the pink petal-covered paths laid out in the sixteenth century by a retired political censor. Ponds seem to adjoin nearly every significant building. Particularly notable are the Hall of the Thirty-six Mandarin Ducks and the Pavilion of Expecting Frost. Don't miss the islands in the lotus pond.

▲▲▲ **Master of Nets Garden**—The kiosks and ponds here attract visitors from all over the world. Reproduced in part at New York's Metropolitan Museum of Art and in miniature at Paris's Pompidou Center, this refuge was the work of a retired twelfth-century bureaucrat who wanted to net the brightest men in Suzhou and enjoy their company.

▲▲ **Surging Wave Pavilion**—One of the city's oldest gardens, this woodsy site is laced by small creeks. Visitors enjoy walking down winding paths that lead past flowering fruit trees to rock gardens with unusual limestone formations. These are Suzhou's Taihu stones, reminiscent of some of the weirdly eroded hoodoos found at Bryce Canyon National Park. According to *Magnificent China*, they were all prematurely aged by a very creative process: tossing them in Lake Taihu and leaving them for several years. The water ate holes in the rocks and made them look like sculpted hunks of Swiss cheese.

▲▲**Garden of Harmony**—Because it's a bit off the beaten track, this nineteenth-century garden is a good choice on a busy Suzhou weekend. It has the traditional pools, small hills, rock gardens, and pavilions. The floral displays are a main attraction, particularly in the spring.

Helpful Hints
Biking in China is not for the faint of heart. Be sure to check the brakes before setting out. Always lock your bike when visiting one of the gardens. Although Suzhou is flat, this is a fairly long ride. Bike traffic can be heavy at times. Be sure to allow extra time to make your train.

Shopping is a major passion in Suzhou. The Youyi Street craft shops between Fenghuang Street and the Suzhou Hotel offer high-quality embroidery, ceramics, fans, and other reasonably priced crafts. While the stores here specialize in take-away items, Suzhou's green thumb brigade is also willing to bring its expertise to your own backyard. One local export company is available to build Suzhou-style gardens complete with pavilions, verandas, bridges, rockeries, and ponds.

DAY 11
SHANGHAI: PEOPLE'S PARK AND CHILDREN'S PALACES

This is a day to leisurely explore one of China's best shopping streets and visit People's Park and the Municipal Children's Palace. You'll also see the Jade Buddha Temple, or, if you prefer, you might take a cruise down the Huangpu.

Suggested Schedule

8:00 a.m.	Breakfast at your hotel.
9:00 a.m.	Stroll down Nanjing Road.
11:00 a.m.	People's Park.
2:30 p.m.	Jade Buddha Temple.
3:00 p.m.	Municipal Children's Palace.
Evening	Dinner and nightlife.

Travel Route
Walk west on Nanjing Road to People's Park. After lunch, catch a taxi to the Jade Buddha Temple. Then taxi to the Municipal Children's Palace at 64 Yan'an Xi Road.

Sightseeing Highlights
▲▲▲ **Nanjing Road**—With more than 350 stores, this is one of the Middle Kingdom's most prosperous shopping streets. Here you'll find some of China's biggest and best arts and crafts stores, bookshops, and pharmacies dispensing herbal medicines. You can shop for woodblock prints and carvings at Pavilion of Clustered Clouds, 422 E. Nanjing Road, or pick up traditional robes, slippers, and silk boots at the Shanghai Opera Costume and Prop Factory, 259 E. Nanjing Road. At the intersection of E. Nanjing Road and Xizang Road, you'll find the No. 1 Department Store (formerly the Sun Company), with more than 1,000 counters selling over 30,000 items. Past People's Park at 190-208 W. Nanjing Road there's a vast selection of wood, stone, jade, and silk items at the Shanghai Arts and Crafts Sales Service Center.

▲▲ **People's Park**—Visit English Corner here on Sunday morning and you'll have a chance to chat with Shanghai residents eager to practice their English. No matter when you come, this park is one of Shanghai's highlights, a place where workers read poetry during breaks and children have the run of handsome gardens. Originally a British racecourse, this 30-acre site is adjacent to People's (or Renmin) Square, Shanghai's answer to Tian'anmen Square in Beijing. Parades are staged here on major holidays. The nearby Park Hotel at 170 Nanjing Road is a good place for lunch (or see the alternative suggested below at Jade Buddha Temple).

▲▲ **Jade Buddha Temple**—Built in 1918, this temple is famous for its white Burmese jade statues that miraculously escaped the cultural purge of the Red Guards. Also notable are statues of the celestial kings and the gilded Buddhas found in the Tianwang Dian Hall. Resident monks run a vegetarian restaurant here.

▲▲ **Municipal Children's Palace**—After the revolution, a dozen of the city's finest mansions were transformed into children's palaces. The one you will visit today at 64 Yan Xi Street, serves as an after-school academy for gifted and talented young musicians, gymnasts, Ping-Pong players, ballerinas, computer nerds, and so forth. No tour of China is complete until you've heard a young violinist play "Oh Susannah" or a precocious tenor sing "Old MacDonald." With luck perhaps you'll hear both during your visit today.

Itinerary Option

A relaxing way to see the Huangpu waterfront is to take the Y15 ($2.85) cruise leaving at 8:30 a.m. and 1:30 p.m. from a Bund dock near the Peace Hotel. This three-hour ride gives you a 36-mile tour of the busy river crowded with everything from junks to ocean liners.

If you haven't had a chance to hear the Peace Hotel Jazz Band or see the Shanghai Acrobatic Theater, consider doing so tonight. Or, if you prefer, attend a performance at the Conservatory of Music, 20 Fenyang Lu, off Huaihai

Road. Phone 437-0137 for show information. The conservatory is located in Frenchtown, one of the handsomest areas in Shanghai.

Incidentally, Huaihai Road in the vicinity of the Jinjiang Hotel is one of the city's most interesting shopping districts. Once part of the French concession, the shops here showcased the finest European styles in colonial days. Today, it remains a good place to shop for fine apparel, shoes, jewelry, pewter, and porcelain.

DAY 12
SHANGHAI TO HONG KONG

Today you depart China for one of the world's great destinations, Hong Kong. Fortunately you're arriving just in time to see the twilight of British rule, set to end in 1997. Although some people visualize Hong Kong as a jam-packed Asian metropolis, it is actually an archipelago of great physical beauty where modern commerce and rural villages coexist peacefully. The contrasts are especially rewarding to tourists, who can sample old and new China tinged with a bit of merry old England. Hong Kong is a wonderful place to shop for bargains, sample new cuisines, or explore remote backcountry villages. This itinerary, which gives you a look at both urban and rural Hong Kong, offers a chance to see some of the colony's greatest assets.

Suggested Schedule

Morning	At leisure in Shanghai.
Noon	Depart for Shanghai Airport.
3:00 p.m.	Depart Shanghai for Hong Kong.
4:30 p.m.	Arrive Hong Kong.
5:30 p.m.	Check into your hotel. Evening at leisure.

Hong Kong
Few cities offer greater contrasts and more diverse opportunities for tourists than Hong Kong. Technically a British crown colony this city of 5.6 million encompasses a little over 1,000 square kilometers. The city is 98 percent Chinese, but there are also healthy smatterings of Vietnamese, Thai Filipinos, Indonesians, Koreans, Japanese, Pakistanis, and Europeans. Most of them live in the business center, Hong Kong Island, and the dense urban factory centers of the Kowloon Peninsula. North toward the Chinese border are the modern new towns of the New Territories. But most of this region and the colony's 235 outlying islands remain a rural outpost where you

Day 12 77

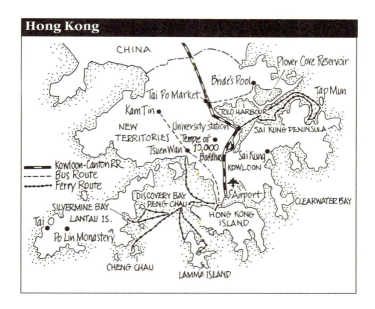

can glimpse traditional Chinese life and visit ancient walled villages.

Although Hong Kong's contemporary image is relentlessly urban, with residents crammed into towering apartment blocks, the colony was a backwater when the British took it over in 1841 during the Opium War. Only 3,650 Chinese lived in the little fishing villages dotting the harbor. Under British dominion, this small outpost gradually expanded its boundaries and became China's commercial link with the world. Ultimately, Hong Kong replaced Shanghai as Southeast Asia's key business center.

Although the colony remains overwhelmingly Chinese today, English is also widely spoken. Hong Kong is the front door to China for businesspeople from all over the world who depend on the city's merchant princes to ease their way into commercial channels in cities like Canton (Guangzhou) and Beijing.

In 1997, when Hong Kong reverts to the Chinese, more than the politics of this city is likely to change. In a sense, Hong Kong is what much of China would like to become, a moderately prosperous Asian land with a dependable industrial base. The colony also has much of the infrastructure that Chinese cities covet—the roads, the subways, and the tourist facilities that meet the standards of demanding foreign visitors. Hong Kong also has an international flavor that brings together the best of East and West and makes it a bit of a novelty among major Asian centers. The city is famous for offering quality goods at very fair prices. As you shop alongside Japanese visitors, who find that cameras made in their own country sell for less in Hong Kong than in Tokyo, you will get a sense of this colony's business acumen.

Although the business centers have been Westernized, you need only turn the corner into a residential neighborhood to be quickly reminded that this is, at heart, a Chinese land where the teachings of Taoism, Confucianism, and Buddhism are the religious order of the day. Of course, the Protestant work ethic holds sway in the small shops that are commonly open twelve hours a day, seven days a week. A seemingly nonstop port town, Hong Kong is also an extremely efficient community, particularly when contrasted to China. While you are visiting this modern city, keep in mind that you are seeing the last of the good old Western-style days. When the Union Jack is lowered in 1997, Hong Kong is destined to become the same—only different.

Arrival
Perhaps the most centrally located major airport in the world, Kai Tak is in the middle of Kowloon, one of Hong Kong's two major population centers. On one approach pattern, the blast from your jet will help dry the laundry hanging from teeming apartment buildings. After clearing customs, stop by the Hong Kong Tourist Association booth to pick up free maps and guides. Then change a small amount of money (you'll probably get a better rate at the banks downtown). For a quick mental conversion from Hong Kong to U.S. dollars, multiply the Hong Kong value by 13 and move the decimal point two places to the left. For example HK$100 equals approximately US$13.

The Hong Kong dollar (HK) is pegged to the U.S. dollar, presently HK$7.8 to US$1. Although cab fares into town are reasonable, there may be a line when you arrive. It may be quicker to take the Airbus (HK$6-$8, or about $.77-$1.02) to your hotel. The only catch is that you won't get any help putting your luggage on board.

Lodging

Hong Kong has an outstanding variety of accommodations in all price ranges. From well-situated YMCAs and mountaintop monasteries to five-star hotels, this city accommodates every taste. Inexpensive hotels run under HK$400 (about $50), moderate hotels run HK$400 to HK$800 ($52-$104), and expensive hotels start around HK $1,000 ($130).

The **YMCA** operates three hotels in the Hong Kong area. Oldest and best known is the branch at 41 Salisbury Road, Kowloon (tel. 3692211; fax 3115809). It's next door to the expensive Peninsula Hotel and across the street from the harbor. Rooms here run HK$500 to HK$670 ($65-$81). Because this hotel is often full, you may want to try the similarly priced **YMCA International House** at 23 Waterloo Road, Kowloon (tel. 7719111, fax 388-5926). On the Hong Kong side, consider the moderately priced **Harbour View International House** at 4 Harbour Road, Wanchai (tel. 5201111; fax 8656063). Rooms run HK$560 to HK$850 ($82-$107). Close by, in roughly the same price range, is the **Harbour** at 116 Gloucester Road (tel. 5748211; fax 5722185).

Naturally, Hong Kong has many fine upscale hotels. One of the best is the **Hotel Victoria,** just steps from the Macau Ferry Terminal and not far from the Outer Islands Ferry Terminal. Rooms run HK$1,450 to $3,450 ($188-$450), and the harbor location at 200 Connaught Road is tops (tel. 5407228; fax 5476912). If you prefer a more remote location, consider the moderate **Surf Hotel** on Sha Ha Beach at Sai Kung, about half an hour by bus from Kowloon. Far removed from the clamor of Hong Kong, this is a charming village. The hotel on Tai Mong Tsai

Road offers swimming, tennis, canoeing, windsurfing, and a good seafood restaurant. Rooms start around HK$422 ($45) a day (tel. 7924411).

On a tight budget? Contact the **Hong Kong Youth Hostels Association** at 1408A Watson's Estate, North Point, Hong Kong (tel. 5706222, or after hours, 8175715). This organization operates hostels on Hong Kong Island and more remote locations, such as the Sai Kung Peninsula and the outer islands. Guest membership and accommodation charges are inexpensive. Some of the outer island hostels have camping facilities. A detailed listing of accommodations is available from the Hong Kong Tourist Association, Shop 8, Basement, Jardine House, 1 Connaught Place C., Hong Kong (tel. 8017177). The association also maintains an office in the airport arrival area.

After settling into your hotel, it's time to begin exploring the city. Hong Kong is perhaps the most accessible city in Asia. The local subway (MTR) is an efficient way to get around town. Cabs are moderately priced (just ask the hotel desk to write out instructions for the driver in Chinese), and there's a good bus and ferry system. In addition, the Kowloon-Canton Railway provides efficient service to the New Territories.

Food
Westerners tend to divide Chinese food up into such familiar categories as Cantonese, Szechuan, and Peking. In fact, there are numerous other categories, such as Shanghai, Chiuchow, and Hakka. All are found in Hong Kong, one of the best and most reasonably priced restaurant towns in the world. While here, you'll certainly want to sample Chiuchow cuisine, famed for its shellfish dishes, such as steamed lobster and crabmeat balls. You might want to order the freshwater "ricefish" hotpot served on a fish-shaped platter or the KuFu tea made at your table. A good place to experiment is the moderately priced **Chiuchow Garden Restaurant**, at Hennessy Centre, 500 Hennessy Road, Causeway Bay (tel. 5773391). For dim sum, the **North Sea Fishing Village** in the basement of Tsimshatsui East's Auto Plaza is a good bet (moderate). Be sure to try the shrimp dumplings (tel. 7236843). Thai food is also a very good bet in Hong Kong, and some of the best is served at the **Chili Club**, a moderately expensive establishment at 68-70 Lockhart Road, Wanchai. Try the spicy chicken or deep-fried fish and chili cakes (tel. 5272872). For ambience, you'll have a hard time beating **Spices**, an eclectic Asian restaurant at 109 Repulse Bay Road, Repulse Bay. It's on our itinerary for Day 13 (tel. 8122711).

On the Kowloon side, the **Spring Deer** restaurant is well known for its Peking duck and clay-baked beggar's chicken, which must be ordered in advance. Dim sum is also available here. It's at 42 Mody Road, Tsim Sha Tsui (tel. 7233673). For European cuisine, try **Jimmy's Kitchen** at Kowloon Center, 29 Ashley Road, Tsim Sha

Tsui (tel. 2684027). Reasonably priced **East Ocean Seafood Restaurant** is another good choice. It's located in East Ocean Centre, 98 Granville Road, Tsim Sha Tsui East (tel. 7238128).

Evening Ideas
If you're staying on the Kowloon side, you might want to explore the Temple Street night market in Kowloon, an Asian bazaar selling all kinds of souvenirs and bargain priced goods. On the Hong Kong side, it's fun to ride one of the old trams from the central district out through Wanchai to the Causeway Bay shopping area on the western end of Hong Kong Island. One of the few areas on this side of the island that hasn't been overwhelmed by high-rises, it features old shops selling Chinese herbs, salted fish, and dried seafood. On your way back to central Hong Kong, stop at Causeway Bay's Food Street, off Gloucester Road, where you'll find many varieties of Chinese food, as well as restaurants specializing in Japanese, Taiwanese, Vietnamese, Spanish, and American cuisine. Vast shopping malls and some of the city's best boutiques are also found in this neighborhood. Many are open until 9:00 p.m. or later. If you want to sample both sides of the harbor, take the Star Ferry, a short ride connecting Kowloon with Hong Kong. It will give you a feel for some of the longer trips you can enjoy in this archipelago aboard the Hong Kong and Yamutai Ferry Company fleet. The ideal way to end your first night here is the tram ride up to the top of Hong Kong's Victoria Peak, where you'll enjoy a panoramic view of this Asian citadel.

DAY 13
HONG KONG: VICTORIA PEAK, STANLEY, AND SHEK-O

Today you'll have a chance to explore the urban and rural sides of one of Asia's best-known islands. After seeing the bustling downtown harbor region, take the Victoria Tram up to the top of Victoria Peak and then walk down the mountain through lush parkland. A short bus ride takes you to an oceanside restaurant and then on to Stanley Village, where you can shop 'til you drop for brand-name luxury goods at distressed prices. A cab ride takes you to the rural village of Shek-O. After exploring the headlands here, walk to a little Chinese village at least a century removed from modern Hong Kong. A bus and subway will take you back downtown for dinner and nightlife.

Suggested Schedule

9:00 a.m.	Explore central Hong Kong.
11:00 a.m.	Tram ride to Victoria Peak and walk down the mountain to Pokfulam Reservoir.
1:00 p.m.	Lunch at Spices at the Repulse Bay Hotel.
2:30 p.m.	Shopping in Stanley.
3:30 p.m.	Cab to Shek-O.
4:00 p.m.	Explore Shek-O area.
5:30 p.m.	Bus and subway back to Central Hong Kong. Evening at leisure.

Travel Route
Your day begins in the Hong Kong Visitors Information Center, where you can obtain maps and brochures that will orient you to the region (tel. 7225555). After walking through the central district, head over to the Victoria Peak Tram Station, one block above the Hilton Hotel on Garden Road. From the top, descend on the Hong Kong Trail to Pokfulam Reservoir, then catch the #73 bus or a cab to Repulse Bay for lunch or continue via bus #73 to Stanley Village for lunch. Afterward take a cab to Shek-O.

Later, take bus #9 to the Shau Kei Wan MTR Station, where the subway will return you to central Hong Kong.

Sightseeing Highlights
Central Hong Kong is a fascinating blend of Asia's new and old. This morning you'll have a chance to explore the central business district and see famous markets, craft and herb shops, and the memorable work of artisans next door to tourist kitsch.

▲**Central Market**—Start your day, as many residents do, at the Central Market, Queen Victoria Street and Des Veoux Road Central. The largest of the city's sixty-five public markets, it has over 300 stalls selling everything from fresh shark to medicinal herbs. Continue on Des Veoux Road across Jubilee Street and you'll be surrounded by tempting street food stalls selling fried dough sticks, bowls of shrimp dumplings, and noodle dishes.

▲**Cloth Alley**—Continue on Des Veoux Road and turn left at Wing On Street. This small street is an excellent place to bargain for shirt fabrics, wool, linen, and velvet. Go right on Queen's Road Central to Wing Sing Street and turn right. Continue to Wing Lok Street and turn left. Turn left again on Man Wa Lane.

▲▲ **Bonham Strand East**—After passing the chop or seal carving shops (you can buy your own seal as a souvenir), turn right on Bonham Strand East. From October to February, the snake shops here are booming. In season, there are always plenty of tasty pythons and cobra to choose from. You'll find restaurants in this area serving snake soup; or, if you prefer, go for a snake banquet, where you can have a shot of snake gall wine, made from the gall bladder. This drink is considered to be just the thing for rheumatism. Or order a glass of snake wine (don't bother ordering the red or white; this liquor made from bile only comes in green). If you miss the snake season, have a look at some of the fascinating medicine shops, which have just the herbs you'll need to balance your yin and yang. There's nearly always an herbalist on duty here.

▲▲▲ **Victoria Peak Tram Tour**—Last night you saw the night view of Hong Kong. Today this same tram is an integral part of our itinerary. It's the easy way to begin your look at the backside of Hong Kong Island. Take a taxi to the tram terminal or retrace your path on Bonham Strand East until it turns into Queen's Road Central. At the Hilton, turn right on Garden Road to the tram. When she's in town, famed travel writer Jan Morris takes her constitutional on this peak. When you reach the top, you'll quickly see why this spot is such a favorite of Hong Kong visitors. A 45-minute walk in either direction takes you around the peak via Harlech and Lugard roads. This is an ideal way to gain perspective on the Hong Kong region. It's also a lot of fun. After enjoying views of the harbor, begin the Hong Kong Trail (the trail sign says Reservoir), which descends 1.2 miles down the mountain spine through the lush country-side to the Pokfulam Reservoir. If you have a couple of days to spare, you could continue on this 30-mile walking route through all five of the island's county parks; but today's walk ends at the

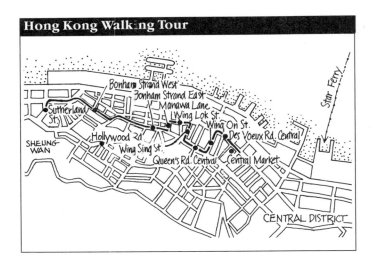

reservoir. Hail a cab on Peak Road or take the #7 bus eastbound and connect to the #73, disembarking at the old Repulse Bay Hotel site, 109 Repulse Bay Road, for lunch.

▲ **Repulse Bay Hotel**—In earlier decades, this white hotel was famous for its whitewashed veranda, where you could sit and enjoy a drink while looking out over one of the island's most popular beaches. To the horror of preservationists, this colonial landmark was demolished in 1982. Fortunately, this establishment has become the Lazarus of the Hong Kong hotel world. Rebuilt on the original oceanfront site, it no longer offers lodging, but you can still enjoy the ambience of this Hong Kong classic at **Spices**, an expensive establishment serving everything from Indonesian *nasi goreng* (rice, chicken, eggs, chilies, and prawns) to a Thai-style chicken curry. Or, if you prefer, just have a look around this historic place and take the #73 bus on to Stanley Village for lunch.

▲ **Stanley**—Popular with bargain hunters, the shops and stalls of Stanley are a good place to look for brand-name garments at considerable savings. Rattanware and Chinese furniture are also sold at factory prices. The village beach is less crowded than the one at Repulse Bay. Take a break at a little British pub called Stanley's, 86 Stanley

Main Street (tel. 8138873). While enjoying lunch in the second floor dining room, you'll have a fine harbor view. You may overhear passionate shoppers at adjacent tables conducting postmortems on their day's outing.

▲▲ **Shek-O**—Many Hong Kong natives have never been to the southwestern tip of their own island. Few tourists have even heard of this area. A ten-minute cab ride from Stanley will take you to this little headland village. The beaches here and at nearby Big Wave Bay are two of the finest in the archipelago. On a clear day you'll enjoy a panoramic view of the Sai Kung Peninsula. A short walk north takes you to an old Chinese settlement. If you have extra time, hike up the Dragon's Back in adjacent Shek-O County Park. This moderately strenuous hike offers fine marine and mountain views. For more information, inquire at the Hong Kong Tourist Association Office. If you don't have time to make it to one of the outer islands, by all means see Shek-O. It will give you a good feel for the colony's village life.

DAY 14
HONG KONG: OUTER ISLANDS

Most people think of Hong Kong as a jam-packed Asian metropolis. In fact, virtually all of the crown colony's 5.6 million residents live either in Kowloon or on Hong Kong Island. Surrounding these two hubs are 235 other islands that comprise the Hong Kong archipelago. From Cheung Chau (population 20,000) to uninhabited islands stretching out into the South China Sea, these retreats are an ideal way to go back in time. Today you'll do just that compliments of the Hong Kong and Yaumati Ferry Company. It costs less than $4 for the ride to your choice of outer islands. The only hard part is choosing among the islands, where you can explore mountaintop monasteries and Buddhist temples, stroll deserted beaches, cycle past rice paddies, dine at fresh seafood restaurants, and shop for Chinese crafts. Of course, if you fall in love with one of these islands, it's usually possible to spend the night.

Suggested Schedule

8:00 to 8:45 a.m.	Arrive at Outlying Districts Ferry Terminal, Hong Kong. Board a vessel for Cheung Chau, Lamma, or Lantau.
10:00 a.m.	Arrive on the island of your choice.
4:00 to 5:00 p.m.	Return to Hong Kong. Evening at leisure.

Transportation

The Outlying Districts Ferry Pier is located on Pier Road off Connaught Road Central. Star Ferry passengers arriving from Kowloon should turn right when they disembark in Hong Kong and walk down to the Outlying Pier. If you're traveling on a weekend or holiday, purchase your ticket in advance. Hotel reservations are also recommended on weekends or holidays. It's a good idea to arrive 15 to 20 minutes before sailing time on weekends, particularly during summer, when the vessels are extremely crowded. Call the ferry company at 5423081 for schedule information (also available from the Hong Kong Tourist Association at tel. 8017177). Purchase a round-trip ticket. Be sure to carry change for exact-fare ferries. Round-trip fares range from HK$10 to HK$30 ($1-$3.84). Don't forget to double check the return ferry times after arriving at your destination.

Sightseeing Highlights: Hong Kong's Outlying Islands
▲▲**Cheung Chau** (suggested departure 8:45 a.m. from Hong Hong Outlying Districts Ferry Pier)—One of the best outings from Hong Kong, this trip is made in the company of locals enjoying a daylong holiday. A highlight is cruising through Hong Kong Harbour, where junks, sampans, freighters, and cruise liners coexist peacefully. After an hour of threading through the Hong Kong archipelago, the ferry slows for the floating neighborhood that bobs about in Cheung Chau Harbour.

About 10 percent of the 20,000 residents on this dumbbell-shaped island just 7.5 miles west of Hong Kong live on junks. Inhabited for over 2,500 years, Cheung Chau emerged as a major port for cities along the South China Coast in the sixteenth century. It was also a haven for pirates, including the infamous Cheung Po Tsai, who hid in a cave on the southwestern side of the island. Today, the island remains a shipbuilding center. Near the pier, you can watch shirtless shipbuilders create these handsome junks without the aid of blueprints. You may also find uniformed schoolchildren tossing balls, old men reading newspapers while sipping tea, and vendors selling barbecued fish on skewers.

On the pier you'll find vendors selling fruit, vegetables, and fresh seafood. One thing you won't find in this village is cars. They are banned on the island, which has preserved many preindustrial traditions and is dominated by clans and trade guilds. A short walk north takes you to Pak Tai Temple, notable for its two excellent stone dragon carvings and a sword forged during the Sung dynasty (A.D. 960-1279). Return to Cheung Chau's Pak She Street and you'll find incense shops, groceries, craftsmen polishing jade, and Gee Jat Po, a paper-bundling shop selling items for funerals. Most of these goods will become part of cremations, helping loved ones prosper in the next world. The rest will be set out on the anniversaries of their deaths.

Just ten minutes east of Cheung Chau Pier is Tung Wan Beach, where windsurfers and swimmers entertain themselves near a large rock adorned with Bronze Age carvings. After pausing for tea at the Warwick Hotel, take Hak Pa Road to Kwun Yum Wan Beach and Kwun Yum Temple, dedicated to its namesake, the Goddess of Mercy. Then return to Fa Feng Road and central Cheung Chau. Following lunch, take a local ferry to Sai Wan, another pleasant waterfront village. Walk up to the temple of Tin Hau, Queen of Heaven and Goddess of the Sea. It's adjacent to the pirate cave of Cheung Po Tsai. Return to Cheung Chau Pier by foot or motorized sampan in time to catch the 4:30 p.m. ferry back to Hong Kong.

Of course, it's also possible to spend the night on the island. Rooms at the comfortable waterfront Cheung Chau Warwick on East Bay are HK$700 ($54) to HK$1,850 ($142) per day (tel. 9810081). More modest accommodations are available at the Cheung Chau Star House, 149 Tai Sun Back Street. Rooms are inexpensive on weekdays and moderate on weekends (tel. 9810101). Advance reservations are always a good idea, particularly on holidays and weekends.

▲▲**Lantau** (suggested departure 8:15 a.m. ferry from Hong Kong Outlying Districts Ferry Pier to Silvermine Bay)—Twice the size of Hong Kong Island, Lantau has less than 16,000 residents. With verdant mountain peaks, ruins of an old fort, traditional Chinese villages, temples, monasteries, and more than 40 miles of trails leading through two country parks, this is an ideal day trip. Inhabited since neolithic times, Lantau's economy centered around fishing, salt-making, and lime-burning for many centuries. Today, tourists eager to see this rugged place make an important contribution to local commerce.

One of the island's most popular beaches is located just five minutes from the ferry dock at Silvermine Bay. You can also explore the area on foot or on a bike rented at the stand in front of the Silvermine Beach Hotel. Head up Mui Wo Rural Committee Road through lush fields and you'll come to Man Mo Temple, which pays homage to both the civil god and the martial god. Adjacent to this landmark is a fabulous mansion with a pagoda-style roof and squadrons of gardeners grooming the estate's topiary garden. The island's old silver mine is a short walk uphill from the mansion.

After returning to the wharf and exploring the Silvermine Bay area, turn in your bike (if you rented one) and catch a bus or taxi to visit the island's leading attraction, the Po Lin Monastery. A pair of two-story temples here feature bronze Buddha statues that are bathed in holy water every May during a Lord Buddha birthday celebration. On an adjacent plateau, you'll see the tallest Buddha statue in Southeast Asia, built at a cost of more than $8 million. Be sure to enjoy the vegetarian lunch served at Po Lin. If you've ever wanted to spend the night at a monastery, this is your chance. Naturally, the boards are harder than what you're used to sleeping on. Inexpensive rooms at Po Lin include three vegetarian meals per day; there are communal bathrooms. Telephone 9855426 or write to the Po Lin Monastery, Ngong Ping, Lantau. Accommodations are also available at the Trappist Haven Monastery northeast of Silvermine Bay. There are numerous campsites to serve hikers on Lantau, as well as a variety of hotels. For a complete list, contact the Hong Kong Tourist Association.

There are many other attractions on Lantau, including Hong Kong's only tea gardens, the nineteenth-century Tung Chung Fort, shipbuilders creating junks and modern yachts on Penny's Bay, and the old salt-panning village of Tai-O. If your image of Asia is homes built on stilts, temples, Buddhist markets, coffin shops, herbal medicine stores, and fishermen unloading their catch onto the town dock, you've come to the right place. Some of the best seafood in the archipelago is found here. Two-mile-long Cheung Sha Beach is another popular Lantau spot. It's 20 minutes by bus from Silvermine Bay.

▲ **Lamma** (suggested departure from Hong Kong Outlying Districts Ferry Pier is 8:35 a.m. to Yung Shue Wan)—Just 40 minutes from Hong Kong, this outer island is prized for its beaches and its ban on cars. Your first stop will be Yung Shue Wan (Banyan Tree Bay), where shops and stalls sell everything from dried fish to candles. There are no big monasteries, but as you walk south across the island you will come to Tin Hau Temple, guarded by a matched pair of granite lions. A strenuous trail beginning at the temple leads up to the peak of 1,100-foot-high Mt. Stenhouse, where there is a fine view of Hong Kong and neighboring islands. Continuing through the fields from Tin Hau Temple, you'll come to one of the island's best beaches, Hung Shing Ye. After relaxing at this popular spot, continue up the road into the hills and you'll be rewarded with a fine view of Lamma, Hong Kong, and several other islands.

Sok Kwu Wan is an excellent place for a seafood lunch or dinner before catching the ferry back to Hong Kong. You might want to try the Cantonese Peach Garden Seafood Restaurant at #11 Sok Kwu Wan Main Street or Man Fung Seafood Restaurant at First St. #5 in Yung Shue Wan. If you want to see more of the island, take the 30-minute walk east along the beach to Mo Tat Wan. It's adjacent to the 300-year-old village of Mo Tat. From here you can return to Sok Kwu Wan and catch the ferry back to Hong Kong. Or, if you prefer, take the local boat across to Aberdeen on Hong Kong Island and then catch a #7 bus back into central Hong Kong.

Other Outer Islands—While Cheung Chau, Lantau, and Lamma are the most visited outer islands, you may also want to stop off en route. Peng Chau, which also endures happily without benefit of automobiles, can be reached as a stopover on the Lantau route. In addition, you can reach Po Toi (pop. 200) on the way to Lamma's Sok Kwu Wan. You'll find plenty of elbow room as well as great views of Hong Kong.

DAY 15
HONG KONG: THE LAND BETWEEN

Your last day in Hong Kong gives you a preview of one of Asia's most important political transformations. In 1997, Britain will retreat from China after 150 years of colonial rule. This, of course, raises the political question of the decade in Asia: will the crown colony become a shadow of its former self like Shanghai? Or will capitalism continue to flourish under Chinese Communist rule? A good place to look for answers is Hong Kong's New Territories, where old walled villages and farms tended by Hakka women are found just a few miles from China's booming new border manufacturing plants. After a tour of this fast-developing region, you'll enjoy lunch on a terrace overlooking Tolo Harbour and then, if you wish, cruise out into this waterway, which resembles a Norwegian fjord.

Suggested Schedule

8:30 a.m.	Join Land Between tour.
9:30 a.m.	Bamboo Forest Monastery, Kowloon.
10:30 a.m.	Hong Kong's highest mountain, Tai Mo Shan, traditional market at Leun Wo, Hong Kong-China border area, Kam Tin walled village.
Noon	Visit Plover Cove County Park.
1:00 p.m.	Lunch at Yucca de Lac.
3:00 p.m.	Return to Hong Kong or cruise Tolo Harbour.
Rest of Day	Shopping, exploring Kowloon or central Hong Kong.

Sightseeing Highlights
▲▲ **Land Between Tour**—At HK$260 ($33.80), this tour of the New Territories is a fine way to get out beyond urban Hong Kong and see the terraced fields, parks, duck ponds, and rural villages on the Chinese border. Named for the area that bridges the gap between old and new Hong Kong, the route offers an excellent introduction to

traditional Chinese village life. The tour can be booked through the Hong Kong Tourist Association Office in Jardine House (tel. 8017177), the information center at the Kowloon Star Ferry Concourse in Tsimshatsui, or the Royal Garden Hotel in Tsimshatsui East. The pickup for the tour is Queen's Pier Central at 8:30 a.m., the Holiday Inn Golden Mile Hotel at 9:00 a.m., or the Holiday Inn Harbour View Hotel at 9:10 a.m. The tour price includes lunch.

Your trip begins with a stop at Chuk Lam Sim Yuen, the Bamboo Forest Monastery, best known for its three Precious Buddha statues. Also here are the Laughing Buddha, the Four Heavenly Kings, the Lord of the Western Paradise, and the 18 Lohans (disciples) of Buddha. On both sides of the main hall is the home for the aged, run by the temple nuns. After contributing $3,000 to $4,000, the elderly can live here for the rest of their lives.

From here, the tour proceeds north to Tai Mo Shan, where you'll get a fine view of Hong Kong before heading down through fish breeding ponds and chicken farms to Luen Wo Market, where stalls offer dried fish, herbs, vegetables, fruit, flowers, meat, and poultry. After passing through a bird sanctuary that's home to Chinese pond herons, you'll continue on to a Hong Kong-China border overlook. In the distance, you'll see China's special incentive zone at Shenzhen, where foreign investment has created vast industrial development. The tour continues through farmland worked by the Hakka women, who tend the fields while their husbands handle domestic chores. You'll ride through mountainous Plover Cove County Park before returning to the market town of Tai Po and your luncheon banquet at the hillside Yucca de Lac restaurant. If you're as impressed by the view of Tolo Harbour as we were, consider leaving the tour at this point and taking a four-hour trip out into this mountain-rimmed bay that resembles the fjords of Norway.

The Land Between tour ends back in Hong Kong about 3:00 p.m.; but if you want to depart from the group after lunch at the Yucca de Lac restaurant, here are options to consider for the balance of the day:

Day 15

▲ **Tolo Harbour Tour**—Just a short distance from the Yucca de Lac by cab is Ma Liu Shui, port for the Tolo Harbour Ferry. This ferry leaves every afternoon at 3:15, returning to Ma Liu Shui at 7:10 p.m. If you're looking for a long, relaxing ride to historic Chinese villages, consider this trip. It's possible to get off at Tap Mun (Grass Island) at 4:50 p.m. and then catch the same ferry back to Ma Liu Shui at 5:50 p.m. If you choose this stopover, be sure to be back at the Tap Mun Pier in plenty of time to catch the 5:50 p.m. boat. It's the last one of the day. Since departure times are subject to change, be sure to confirm the entire ferry schedule in the "Places of Interest by Public Transport" brochure available from the Hong Kong Tourist Association Office. When you reach Ma Liu Shui, a ten-minute walk will take you across a bridge to University Station, where you can catch the train back into Kowloon. Incidentally, you don't have to take the Land Between tour to see Tolo Harbour. Just catch the Kowloon-Canton line at Kowloon Railway Station. Get off at University Station and walk over to the ferry dock at Ma Liu Shui. In addition to the 3:15 p.m. trip, a morning Tolo Harbour run departs Ma Liu Shui at 7:25 a.m. and returns at 11:05 a.m.

▲ **Bride's Pool**—Located in Plover Cove County Park, this landmark is easily reached by cab from the Tai Po Station on the Kowloon-Canton Railway line (about HK$40, or $5). A pleasant mile-long trail will take you past this series of romantic waterfalls. When you're finished, catch the #75K bus back to Tai Po and pick up the Kowloon-Canton Railway back into Kowloon.

▲ **Kam Tin**—A popular New Territories stop, this is the best known of Hong Kong's five walled villages. You can reach Kam Tin by taking a taxi direct from the Yucca de Lac restaurant. A less expensive but more time consuming route is to take a taxi from Yucca de Lac to University Station, where you can take the Kowloon-Canton Railway train back to the MTR and connect to Tsuen Wan Station. Then pick up the #51 bus from the stop above the station on Tai Ho North Road for the 40-minute ride out to Kam Tin.

According to Hong Kong author Barry Girling, this is the crown colony's largest precolonial historical monument and military fortification. Today it is home to 400 descendants of the Tang dynasty, during which it was founded more than 300 years ago. Communities such as Kam Tin were designed to protect the Chinese from pirates, brigands, and other invaders. They were also an occasional refuge for former aristocrats, such as the last members of the Sung dynasty, who took shelter here. The village is entered through an old gate that was seized by the British in 1898 and ceremoniously restored as a token of goodwill 27 years later. Hakka women wearing their black hats and smoking long pipes will gladly pose for about a dollar. Exploring the back streets here, you'll have a chance to visit ancestral halls, a shady market, and small shops. Some of the streets in this tiny town are barely wide enough for a bicyclist. In the evening, you might want to check out a walled village hot spot called the Sweet Garden Night Club.

▲ **Temple of Ten Thousand Buddhas**—If you're feeling energetic, get off the Kowloon-Canton Railway at Shatin and take the half-hour walk to this landmark, where you'll find 12,800 statues of Buddha. A strenuous walk to the top of the pagoda will give you a memorable view of the New Territories.

▲ **Factory Outlets**—People come from all over the world to shop at Hong Kong's factory outlets. Dozens of reputable firms manufacturing designer apparel, leather goods, jewelry, silk goods, beaded track suits, and perfume are listed in the Hong Kong Tourist Association's brochure on this subject. The crown colony also has some of the world's best bargains on computer software. They're found at the Golden Shopping Arcade. Take the MTR to Sham Shui Po, where the station agent can direct you to this computer mall.

▲ **Tea at the Peninsula**—The Peninsula, one of Asia's most elegant hotels, is located near the Kowloon waterfront, just a short walk from the Star Ferry Terminal. The lobby of this Hong Kong landmark is an ideal place to rest after a hard day of sightseeing. Tomorrow you'll head on to either Thailand or Bali. If you have chosen the Thailand option, please turn to Option A on the next page. If you are bound for Bali, turn ahead to Option B.

DAYS 16 TO 22: OPTION A
THAILAND

From the hills and jungles of the Golden Triangle, through the teeming urban metropolis of Bangkok, to the white sand beaches and turquoise waters of its southern peninsula, Thailand is one of the most diverse and complex countries in Asia. Known to many Westerners only through *The King and I* stereotypes, Thailand is a many-faceted society held together in an intricate web of history, culture, religion, and political independence.

Occupying the central and western part of the Indochina Peninsula, with Burma to the west, Laos to the north, Kampuchea to the east, and Malaysia to the south, Thailand is about the size of France, or California and New York combined. Its mountainous north, geologically linked to the great Himalayan range, slopes down into a semiarid northeastern plateau and a fertile central plain. The country is squeezed into a narrow isthmus in the south, bordered by the Gulf of Thailand and the Andaman Sea. Thailand's tropical climate supports a tremendous variety of vegetation (including over 1,000 varieties of orchids) and animals—elephants, tigers, snakes, birds, and monkeys. While the country's economy is being modernized rapidly, exporting tin, rubber, and textiles, three-quarters of the population works in agriculture, mostly related to rice production. Bangkok is a major hub of Asian travel, with all the amenities and symptoms of a modern city; yet much village life remains insulated from twentieth-century civilization.

Thailand's weather pattern falls into three seasons: warm and dry from mid-October to early March (temperatures from 75 to 90 degrees, coolest in December and January); rainy from mid-May to mid-October (wettest in September); hot and dry from March to mid-May (with temperatures reaching 100 degrees). Fall monsoons can limit travel in the south, but the rainy season is not necessarily troublesome for travelers, as the drenching rains tend to come and go in spurts separated by warm, sunny stretches.

The history of Thailand, known as Siam until 1939, is the story of independent Asian civilizations—ancient cultures of the Chao Phraya River Basin, the southern peninsula, and the northern mountains—gradually merging into a unified society. Starting in 1239 during the century-long reign of the Sukhothai kingdom (the "dawn of happiness"), Thais were first united under a single monarch, King Ramkamhaeng, and a single religion, Theravada Buddhism. There followed a succession of kingdoms, including the great Ayutthaya era in the seventeenth century, and encounters with foreigners, notably aggressive Burmese rulers and influential French traders. In 1782, General Chakri, crowned Rama I, moved the Siamese capital to Bangkok and founded the royal dynasty that endures to the present.

Foreign trade flourished in the mid-1800s, but, unlike all of its neighbors, Siam was never governed by an imperial power, and political independence and cultural integrity were important factors in preserving Thailand's unique character. In 1932, a bloodless coup, the first of many throughout the twentieth century, led to the establishment of a constitutional monarchy, governed by a prime minister but strongly shaped by the military. The latest coup took place in early 1991 with the military promising to install a new civilian government.

Thailand's ethnically mixed population of 60 million descends mostly from Mon, Khmer, and Thai peoples but has absorbed waves of migration from China as well. Ninety-five percent of the people are Buddhist, and men typically spend at least three months in the monkhood as they become adults. The abiding spirituality influences the Thai people's universally kind and friendly demeanor. Everywhere you will meet people who go out of their way to make you feel welcome. In return, you can observe a few simple customs. It is impolite to touch people, including children, on their heads or to sit with the soles of your feet pointing at another person. Buddhist monks are not allowed to touch women and will sometimes refrain from social contact with them altogether. The royal family is the object of great affection in Thailand, and respectful behavior is expected of foreigners. Losing one's temper is virtually taboo. The Thai people seem to live by the wisdom of *mai pen rai*, which can be translated as "it doesn't matter" but which actually implies a much deeper acceptance of the moment.

The tonal Thai language is extremely difficult to master. Pronunciation is so complex and crucial that phrase books tend to be of little help. But as tourism has become the country's major industry, giving rise to an efficient infrastructure of plane, train, bus, and taxi transportation, most people involved with travelers speak some English and make great efforts to help visitors enjoy their country.

DAY 16: HONG KONG TO BANGKOK

Home of some of Asia's most beautiful palaces, Bangkok is a gilded city of canals, temples, and reclining Buddhas. From colorful silk to fiery seafood, Bangkok's pleasures belong on any Asian itinerary. Today you will get an overview of this society shaped by Siamese kings and Buddhist priests. Like Kyoto and the Forbidden City, this royal capital is the kind of place you'd expect to find at the end of a yellow brick road.

Suggested Schedule

6:00 a.m.	Leave your hotel for Hong Kong's Kai Tak Airport.
8:00 a.m.	Depart Hong Kong for Bangkok.
10:00 a.m.	Arrive in Bangkok.
11:30 a.m.	Check into your hotel.
Noon	Lunch.
1:00 p.m.	Temple and Grand Palace tour.
7:00 p.m.	Dinner.

Bangkok

The greater metropolitan area of Thailand's largest city covers 580 square miles and is home to over five million

Days 16 to 22: Option A

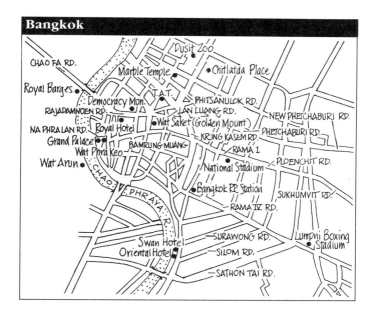

people, almost one-tenth of the country's population. Bangkok's contradictory potpourri of ancient temples and high-rise hotels, quiet canals and frenetic expressways, tranquil saffron-robed monks and hustling drivers of *tuk-tuks* (motorized versions of the old three-wheeled pedicabs) is enough to warrant Thailand's reputation as the most exotic city in Asia. Since King Rama I made it the country's capital in the late eighteenth century, Bangkok has grown into a city that is at once magnificent and mad. The old "Venice of the East" a maze of canals (*klongs*) supporting fishermen and floating markets, is now traversed by bustling avenues carrying 90 percent of Thailand's automobile traffic. Look up from the congested streets to the sharply curving spires of an ancient temple and understand why the Thais call their capital city "Krung Thep," the "City of Angels." In a noisy sidewalk café, dip into a spicy seafood soup or a hot chicken curry and be transported into a paradise of exotic aromas and flavors.

Bangkok proper is bordered by the curving Chao

Phraya River on the west. The Old Royal City was built next to the water. The Dusit District, with the new royal palace, government buildings, and zoo, developed under King Rama V, is just to the northeast of the Old Royal City, across the Klong Phadung. "Modern" Bangkok, where you find many of the new hotels, towering office buildings, and exclusive shops, extends to the south and east along New Petchburi, Sukhumvit, and Silom roads. The combination of Western influences and Asian traditions and the imposition of helter-skelter modern development on an ancient culture that in many ways is still thriving make Bangkok wild, forboding, exciting, and endlessly intriguing.

Getting Around

After clearing immigration and customs, you'll want to head to the bank desk and change at least $20. The exchange rate is 25.3 baht to $1 or 1 baht = $0.04. For a quick mental conversion, multiply the baht amount by 4 and then move the decimal point two places to the left. Thus, a 60 baht dish at a restaurant is worth about $2.40.

One of the first things you notice about Bangkok is the traffic, a mad swirl of speeding cars, trucks, buses, motorbikes, bicycles, and tuk-tuks. Only the bravest of short-term visitors would rent a vehicle and venture out into the apparent chaos. The set taxi fare for the 30-minute ride from the airport into downtown Bangkok is 300 baht ($12). You can leave the airport and bargain a private driver down to 150 to 200 baht ($6-$8), or inquire about a minibus to your hotel for about 100 baht ($4).

Fortunately, Bangkok has a well-developed bus system and a seemingly inexhaustible supply of taxis and tuk-tuks. Buses cost 2 baht (about $.08) for short local trips, 5 to 20 baht ($.20-$.80) for longer crosstown routes. Taxi fares are negotiable—bargain before you get in. The ride from the airport to downtown should cost about 200 baht ($8). Tuk-tuks provide both the cheapest transport and the most down-to-earth views of the city. They, too, are negotiable, starting at 10 baht ($.40) for the shortest

(2- or 3-block) rides. Boats can be hired along the riverbank for about 300 baht ($12) per hour, regardless of the number of passengers.

Travel Route
From the Royal Hotel, turn left (south) down Rachini Road (on the far side of the canal). At Bamrung Muang Road, turn right (west) and at the end of the block you will see the tall, white walls of the Grand Palace. The entrance is around to the right on Naphralan Road.

From either the Oriental or Swan Hotel, take a bus, taxi, or tuk-tuk to the Grand Palace. Or take a jetboat up the Chao Phraya River to the dock near Naphralan Road and walk straight ahead to the Grand Palace.

On leaving the Grand Palace, turn left (west) and walk along Naphralan Road, turning left (south) again on Maharaj Road. Walk along the west wall of the Grand Palace grounds until you reach Charoen Krung Road. Turn left (east). The entrance to Wat Po is in the middle of the block. Return to your hotel by tuk-tuk; there are always several waiting outside the temples.

Sightseeing Highlights
▲▲▲ **Grand Palace**—Here is the one sight that best captures the checkered history, royal splendor, and religious symbolism of premodern Bangkok. Construction on the sprawling grounds was initiated by King Rama I when he moved the country's capital to Bangkok in 1782. The compound includes the palace buildings, a model of the magnificent Khmer temple at Angkor Wat, and the spectacular Temple of the Emerald Buddha. Among the royal buildings is the Chakri Maha Prasat, the British-designed royal residence built for Rama V. It features an Italianate facade and a three-tiered Thai roof. The Dusit Maha Prasat, or audience hall, was built under Rama I in 1789. Next door is the Aphon Phimok Pavilion, or king's disrobing pavilion. Guides at the entrance offer their services for about 450 baht (18), but you can easily tour the grounds yourself with the pamphlet provided at the gate.

The Grand Palace is open daily 8:30 a.m. to 11:30 a.m. and 1:00 p.m. to 3:30 p.m. Admission is 125 baht ($5). Telephone 222-8181, ext. 40.

▲▲▲ **Wat Phra Keo**—Located in the Grand Palace complex, the Temple of the Emerald Buddha is deservedly one of Bangkok's two most famous temples—out of more than 400. Rama I built this remarkable chapel to enshrine the legendary Emerald Buddha image brought down from northern Siam. The image, actually carved from jasper, was discovered in Chiang Rai in 1434 when lightning cracked open an old *chedi* (spire pagoda). It stands less than two-and-a-half-feet high and is enthroned in a towering altar. With the turning of each of Thailand's three seasons, the king ascends the altar and changes the statue's costume. Nearly overshadowed by the gloriously detailed chapel, which features reflecting glass chips, blue tile, and great interior murals of the Ramakien (the Thai version of India's Ramayana story), it nonetheless remains the most sacred of the country's Buddha images.

Wat Pho—The oldest temple-monastery complex in Bangkok, Wat Pho (also known as Wat Phra Jetupon) is most famous for its immense Reclining Buddha. The grounds are a maze of chapels, pavilions, Buddha images, chedis, and marble reliefs. The complex is fascinating but does not adequately prepare you for what you see when you enter the sixteenth-century Temple of the Reclining Buddha. Occupying nearly the entire structure, the figure of Buddha lying on his side is 145 feet long and 50 feet high; it is built of plaster-covered brick and plated with gold leaf. The soles of its feet are inlaid with 108 mother-of-pearl images of the auspicious signs of Buddha. The temple was enlarged and remodeled in 1789 by Rama I and has been undergoing constant reconstruction and repair in recent years. Wat Pho is open daily 8:00 a.m. to 5:00 p.m. Admission is 15 baht ($.60). Tel. 222-0933.

A little-known amenity at Wat Pho are the 80 baht ($3.20) massages offered by students of the temple's massage school. This is one of the few massage parlors in Bangkok we can recommend without reservation. Ask at the entrance.

Lodging
As the travel hub of Southeast Asia, Bangkok offers a mind-boggling variety of accommodations, from the most minimal dormitory-style rooms to the splendor of grand hotels. The legendary jewel in the crown is the **Oriental Hotel** at 48 Oriental Avenue, New Road, Bangkok, 10500. Its over 400 rooms are beautifully appointed, and the lavishly adorned hotel overlooks the Chao Phrang River. The rates—6,000 to 65,000 baht ($240-$2,600)—reflect the Oriental's luxury and its status (tel. 236-0400). Another good bet is the **Regent** at 155 Ratcha Damri Road (tel. 251-6127). This handsome establishment offers rooms starting at 5,000 baht ($200). Upscale and conveniently located is the **Royal Orchid Sheraton** at 2 Captain Bush Lane, Siphaya Road (tel. 234-5599). Just down the street from the Oriental, it offers rooms for 4,800 to 6,000 baht ($192-$240).

More reasonably priced and convenient to old Bangkok and the Grand Palace is the **Royal Hotel** (tel. 222-9111) at 2 Rajadamnern Avenue. Its 300 rooms are clean and comfortable, the staff is helpful, and the large, bustling lobby has a heady international atmosphere. Rates are 956 to 1,295 baht ($38-$52). Our mid-range readers have responded enthusiastically to this establishment. Ask for a room away from the street. The **Swan Hotel,** at 31 Custom House Lane, Charoen Krung Road, directly behind the Oriental, is a good economy accommodation with funky decor and low rates (tel. 234-8594). Rooms are 550 baht ($22). The **New Trocadero** at 343 Surawong Road (tel. 234-8920) is also well priced. Rooms run 1,200 to 1,800 baht ($48-$72).

Low-priced guest houses can be found in the Baglamphu District along Khao San Road just north of the Democracy Monument. The **PB Guest House** (74 Khao

San Rd.), for instance, charges only 60 baht (about $2.50) for a double room with fan and shared bath. **My House** at 37 Soi Ram Buttri (tel. 282-9673) offers doubles for 120 baht ($4.80).

Food
Dining will undoubtedly be one of your most memorable activities in Thailand. Becoming the culinary rage the world over, Thai cuisine takes relatively simple ingredients—white rice (steamed or "sticky"), pork, beef, poultry, seafood, herbs, and spices—and creates soups and main course dishes that are amazingly complex. The sumptuous curries sometimes literally bring you to tears, especially when the fiery native chilis are used in abundance in conjunction with garlic and ginger. Lemon grass, coriander, shrimp paste, fish sauce, and tamarind sauce add to the astonishing mix of flavors.

Although Bangkok caters to every national taste, it would be a crime to ignore the superb native cooking available in all price ranges, from the thousands of street vendors to resplendent restaurants. A cornucopia of sweets is concocted from eggs, beans, rice flour, roots, seeds, palm sugar and coconut. The selection of Thai fruits includes bananas, pineapples, oranges, mango, papaya, sapodilla mangosteen, rambutan, jack fruit, pomelo, and rose, custard, and crab apples.

Such luxury hotels as the **Oriental,** the **Imperial,** and the **Shangri-la** offer fabulous spreads, but we've had splendid meals in the moderately priced restaurants. **Silom Village,** 286 Silom Road between Pramual and Pun roads, is part of a tourist-oriented trade center; yet the patio restaurants offer fresh seafood and mouth-watering curries at reasonable prices. For less than 250 baht ($10), two people can gorge on dry beef curry, chicken-coconut milk soup, green and red curry dishes, and other tempting delicacies. **Vijit** at the corner of Rajadamnern Klang Avenue and **Prachathiptai** near the Democracy Monument are popular and noisy. (A musical combo plays loud pop music.) But the chili oil prawns and garlic, chicken curry, and other dishes are well worth the clamor. The **Whole Earth Restaurant**, at 93/3 Soi Langsuan, Ploenchit Road, serves vegetarian dishes starting at 70 baht ($2.80) for lunch, as well as a wide range of beautifully prepared nonvegetarian soups and curries. One afternoon, looking for a fast lunch, we slipped into the **Sky-High Restaurant**, around the corner from the Royal Hotel. It may have looked like an ordinary coffee shop, but we were served an extraordinary charcoal-fired pot of hot and sour prawn soup for 100 baht ($4), indicative of the delicious, individually prepared dishes available all over the city. If you have a cast-iron stomach and a sense of adventure, try eating from street corner carts, but first seek advice on how to order from a local resident. The **Sala Rim Nara** across the river from the Oriental Hotel offers an elegant $12 buffet. The food and views are great. Take the ferry over from the Oriental dock. Directly behind the Holiday Inn on Silom Road is **Ban Chiang Soy Sriving** (tel. 2367045), which has classic authentic Thai food in a beautiful house for 250 baht ($10).

There are many famous and farang (Western)-oriented restaurants in Bangkok, such as the increasingly popular **Cabbages and Condoms**, operated by the Thai Population Development Association at 10 Soi 12 Sukhumvit Road, but you will have a hard time finding budget dining in such a pleasant setting as the **Kaloang Home Kitchen** at 2 Sri Ayutthaya. (tel. 281-9228). Just have your hotel write down the address in Thai and give it to your taxi driver. This open-air restaurant tucked into a neighborhood at the end of Sri Ayutthaya is near the National Library. A full range of Thai dishes, many quite spicy, is offered—curries, fish dishes, chicken salads—and small longtail boats cruise up to the dock and sell dried squid reconstituted on a charcoal grill. Go in the late afternoon as the sun is setting and enjoy the view of boats moving up and down the river, birds flitting around the piers and bushes, and a genuinely down-home atmosphere for less than 150 baht ($6) per person.

In the same price range is **Somboon Po Chana**, 22-28 Soi Chula 60. It's located in the Samyan District just off Phaya Thai Road (tel. 2515653). Here you'll find wonderful seafood, including curried crab, iron pot shrimp, and grilled calamari. We also recommend **Lemongrass** at #5/1 Sukhumvit Road, Soi 24. A full meal for two runs about $10. For the best breakfast beignets (fried dough) this side of New Orleans, head for the alley just up Surowang Road from the New Trocadero Hotel. They're served each morning from a food cart.

Nightlife

Bangkok is notorious as a wide-open city when it comes to nightlife, a reputation enhanced by the presence of more than a quarter of a million hostesses, escorts, bar girls, and masseuses. Some say that the sex industry is the largest single component of Thailand's tourist business. The most intense concentration of nightclubs, go-go bars, gay clubs, and massage parlors is in the Patpong District, along Patpong I, II, and III, between Silom and Suriwongse roads, and along Soi Cowboy, between Soi 21 and 23 off Sukhumvit Road. Barkers on the street, as well as tuk-tuk and taxi drivers, often hand out small cards listing the types of attractions, including sex acts, available in different clubs. If this is your type of scene, however, remember that tourists are sometimes viewed as easy marks for hustlers and con artists.

Bangkok also offers a wide variety of more conventional and less risky entertainment for foreign travelers. Cultural shows, featuring traditional costumes and classical dances, are presented at most of the big hotels, at the Silom Village Trade Center, and at such restaurants as **Baan Thai** (7 Sukhumvit Soi 32), **Ala Norasing** (Sukhumvit Soi 4), and **Tump-Nak-Thai** (131 Ratchadaphisek Rd.).

Thai boxing, the acrobatic form of fighting in which everything goes but head-butting, is a popular attraction. Since the fights take place with the accompaniment of traditional music, they are like a cross between martial arts and modern dance. They are held at the Lumpini

Stadium on Rama IV Road on Tuesday, Friday, and Saturday evenings at 6:00 p.m., with a Saturday matinee at 1:30. Seats are from 30 to 150 baht ($1.20-$6). At Rajadamnoen Stadium, on Rajadamnoen Nok Avenue, matches are held on Mondays, Wednesdays, and Thursdays at 6:00 p.m. and Sundays at 5:00 p.m. and 8:00 p.m.; admission is 125 to 550 baht ($5-$22).

Helpful Hint
The Tourist Authority of Thailand, or T.A.T., has its head office at #4 Rajadamnoen Nok Avenue (tel. 282-1143-7) and can provide pamphlets, brochures, and reams of helpful information about Bangkok and the rest of Thailand.

DAY 17: BANGKOK

Next to the tranquillity offered by the courtyards and chapels of Bangkok's temples, the most peaceful respite from the city's wild disorder is on its many waterways. Before the building booms of the twentieth century, the canals, or klongs, were such an important part of Bangkok's transportation system that the city was known as the Venice of the East.

Suggested Schedule	
6:00 a.m.	Rise for early breakfast.
7:00 a.m.	River cruise to visit Wat Arun and the Royal Barges.
Noon	Lunch.
1:00 p.m.	Waterway boat tour of Bangkok's klongs.
5:00 p.m.	Relax at your hotel.
7:00 p.m.	Dinner and Thai classical dancing.

Getting Around
Nearly every tourist hotel in Bangkok has a tour information desk or a tour program of its own which includes trips to Wat Arun and the Royal Barges. Regular tours leave the Oriental Hotel pier daily at 7:00 a.m. and return

around 11:00 a.m. The Supatra Company, Ltd., at 254 Arun Amarin Road, Thonburi, arranges single- and double-deck riverboat cruises with set destinations or custom itineraries. In addition to water taxis that cruise the klongs on a regular basis, smaller, speedy longtail boats (*hang yao*) can be chartered for about 200 to 300 baht ($8-$12) per hour. Boats can be hired at the Oriental Hotel pier, at the landing near Silapakorn University in the Grand Palace section of the city, at the Ekamai Bridge on Soi 63, Sukhumvit Road, and at Prakanong Klong Tan Bridge on Soi 71, Sukhumvit.

Sightseeing Highlights

▲▲▲ **Wat Arun**—Located across the Chao Phraya River from Bangkok, in the sister city of Thonburi, the Temple of Dawn is one of the most memorable sights in this metropolis of dazzling physical wonders. It is just southwest of Wat Po and the Grand Palace. In the early nineteenth century, King Rama II decided to expand an earlier temple, Wat Chaeng, established by King Taksin on the site. Wat Arun, with a 282-foot-tall central spire (*prang*) derived from Khmer religious architecture, is the result of his vision. Raised on a series of terraces above the soft ground of the riverbank, the spire is embedded with colored Chinese porcelain and shards of crockery. The grounds include four small corner prangs, four pavilions housing Buddha images, and many statues. Staircases up the tower lead to a commanding view of the river and the surrounding area. In the misty early morning hours, the beautiful silhouette of the spire earns the temple its name. Admission is 5 baht ($.20).

▲▲▲ **The Royal Barges**—Housed in a shed on Klong Bangkok Noi, upriver north of Wat Arun, the Royal Barges are elaborately carved boats that were used in state ceremonies until 1967. At the end of the rainy season, the king would bring gifts across the river from the palace to the Buddhist monks at Wat Arun. The oldest and most ornate of the barges is Sri Supannahong, a fantastic vessel with tiered umbrellas and a marvelous golden pavilion. A crew of 60 was needed to sail it. The last time the barges were put into action was during the centennial of the Chakri dynasty in 1982. Admission is 15 baht ($.60). The shed is open daily from 8:30 a.m. to 4:30 p.m. (tel. 424-0004).

Itinerary Option: Floating Market at Damern Saduak

An hour southwest of Bangkok by car or bus, this water market is famous for its selection of native fruits and vegetables. While it takes longer to reach than its counterpart in Thonburi, this indigenous market is not as tainted by tourism. Damern Saduak is often included in all-day tours that take visitors to the Bridge on the River Kwai in Kanchanaburi and the great chedi in Nakhon Pathom. Other tour packages include an afternoon trip to the Rose Garden, a theme park of traditional handicrafts, regional dances, and elephant shows.

Helpful Hint

If you've made too many purchases to carry with you on the rest of your trip, or if you just want to travel lighter, the cosmetic terminal of the Bangkok airport provides luggage storage for 20 baht ($.80) per day. Check your extra bags or boxes and pick them up when you make your final return to Bangkok.

DAY 18: CHIANG MAI

Today you slip away from the twentieth-century civilization and clamor of Bangkok to land in another world altogether. In the northern hill country, odd-shaped, forested mountains rise from the sloping plains. Rivers and waterfalls course through the jungle terrain. Tribal villages cling to traditional customs. Visiting Thailand's second largest city, you will come in contact with people whose culture is much closer to nineteenth-century ways of life.

Suggested Schedule

8:00 a.m.	Breakfast at hotel and check out.
9:00 a.m.	Taxi to Bangkok Airport for 11:45 a.m. flight
12:45 p.m.	Arrive in Chiang Mai.
1:30 p.m.	Check into hotel or guest house. Lunch.
2:30 p.m.	Explore Chiang Mai and investigate trek and tour options.
7:00 p.m.	Dinner.

Chiang Mai

When King Mengrai was looking for a new capital for his kingdom in 1296, he came upon an auspicious location where two white sambars, two white barking deer, and five white mice were seen together. Chiang Mai ("new town") developed into the "Rose of the North." Located 450 miles north of Bangkok on the banks of the Ping River, Chiang Mai was the great city of the north, the civilization center of Lanna Thai, the "land of the rice fields." From the late sixteenth through the late eighteenth centuries, its power declined, but it began a rebirth in 1796 under the increasing influence of Siam. The old part of the city is still surrounded by a two-hundred-year-old moat and fortified gates, while development has expanded the city in every direction. Still an important center of trekking activity (which has shifted somewhat to Chiang Rai), increasingly popular with tourists, Chiang Mai remains a unique and charming city, still reflecting the Burmese and, to a lesser extent, Laotian influences that shaped much of its history, art, and architecture. During the months of October through January, it is the focus of many religious and cultural festivals.

Although it is Thailand's second largest city, Chiang Mai (pop. 150,000) is only one-fortieth the size of Bangkok's metropolitan area and retains many of its attractive small town features. Most of the temples, shops, hotels, and restaurants are within an area of less than four square miles.

Days 16 to 22: Option A

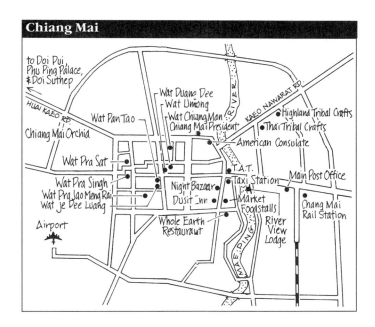

Getting Around

If you choose a hotel or guest house along the Ping River or on nearby Chang Khlan Road, most of Chiang Mai is readily accessible on foot. Tuk-tuks can be hired, starting at 40 baht ($1.60), to take you to specific sites or on tours of your own choice. There are also minibuses and taxis for hire all over the city at negotiable rates, from 60 baht ($2.40) for a short trip, 250 to 500 baht ($10-$20) for all-day tours. At the taxi stand on the corner of Tha Phal and Chang Khlan roads, drivers pick up passengers headed for the same destinations. Four main bus routes crisscross the city and extend into the countryside. The inner city buses are yellow, and the fare is only 2 baht. Bicycle and motorbike rentals are available around most hotels and guest houses. For day tours to the north, simply contact one of the many tour companies around each hotel and guest house. **Mai Ping Leisure Tours**, 95/8 Nimmanhemin Road (opposite the Rincome Hotel) is a professional and friendly operation (tel. 215-126). **Bamboo Tour** (tel.

236-501), **S.T. Tours & Travel** (tel. 212-829), **Meo Tour Services** (tel. 235-116), **Chiang Mai Honey Tour** (tel. 234-345), and **Lamthong Tour** (tel. 235-448) are just a few of scores of trek and tour services available.

Lodging

Consistent with its burgeoning tourist trade, Chiang Mai offers a full range of accommodations, from high-rise hotels to humble guest houses. The **Dusit Inn**, at 112 Chang Khlan Road, has 200 rooms, a swimming pool, restaurants, and a nightclub. It is located on the street where the night bazaar is held. Rates are 2,300 to 9,600 baht ($92-$384). Telephone 281-033. The **Chiang Mai Orchid**, at 100-102 Huay Kaew Road, is one of several high-rise luxury hotels on the outskirts of town. In addition to 267 rooms, it has a pool, restaurants, disco, convention facilities, and a shopping arcade. Rates are 1,210 to 9,680 baht ($48-$240). Tel. 222-099. Probably the best upscale choice away from the increasing congestion of central Chiang Mai is the **Rincome Hotel**, beyond the Chiang Mai Orchid on Huay Kaew Road. The hotel is near the Nantawan shopping arcade and one of our favorite restaurants, Hong Tauw Inn. Rooms run 2,300 to 2,500 baht ($92-$100). If you want deluxe comfort with local touches, your money is well spent here. (Tel. 221-044, 221-130.)

Within the walls of the old city, you'll find **Gap's House**, an economical and homey compound of 18 rooms popular with UNESCO and foreign embassy officials. The singles are 175 baht ($7), doubles are 350 baht ($14), and suites are 550 baht ($22). Arranged in a garden setting and furnished with teak antiques, the rooms are comfortable. Although the dining room serves only breakfast, the owner often invites guests to join him in family-style lunch. Bicycles are provided free. 3 Rajadamnern Road, Soi 4. (Tel. 278-140.) One of the newer additions to Chiang Mai's guest houses is the **River View Lodge** at 25 Charoenprathet Road, Soi 2. Clean, beautifully appointed rooms with fans or air-conditioning overlook tidy gardens and the Ping River. It has an attractive patio restaurant near the river and a pool. Rates are 1,000 to 1,200 baht ($40-$48) with breakfast. If you don't get in here, try the **Galare Guest House** next door at 7 Charoenprathet Road with rooms for about 480 baht ($19.20). Tel. 233-885. The **Chiang Mai Guest House,** 91 Charoenprathet Road, accommodates travelers on more modest budgets with 28 rooms, from dorm style to air-conditioned doubles, at 180 to 420 baht ($7.20-$16.80). Tel. 276-501. **Daret Guest House** at 4/5 Chaiyaphum Road offers rooms for 80 to 120 baht ($4 to $5). It's across the moat from the Daret Restaurant on Moon Muang Road, and you can book treks here.

Food

The cuisine of northern Thailand, influenced by Burma, has subtle differences in spices from that of southern regions. The **Hong Tauw Inn** across from the Rincome Hotel just off Huay Kaew Road offers specialties like hearts of coconut with sweet basil and shrimp, deep-fried Chiang Mai sausage, grilled pork salad, and catfish curry for about 50 to 80 baht ($2-$3.20). For a beautiful outdoor setting on the banks of the Ping River, try **Once Upon a Time**. Located south of the night bazaar at 385/2 Charoenprathet Road, it features shrimp with paprika seeds, red curry with beef and potatoes, and winged bean salad at 200 to 250 baht ($8-$10). The food is great, the service uneven. The **River View Lodge** serves special Chiang Rai dinners upon request. The **Whole Earth** serves impeccably prepared vegetarian and nonvegetarian dishes, curries, soups, and seafood in a pleasant Thai-style elevated restaurant on Sri Dornchai Road. Chiang Mai is full of small restaurants and cafés, as well as tantalizing food stalls, such as those on Loi Kroa Road between Charoenprathet Road and Chang Khlan Road. Popular with Westerners are the **Riverside Cafe** on Charoen Rat Road overlooking the Ping River, the **Thai German Dairy** restaurant at the intersection of Moon Muang Road and Soi 2, and the **Daret Restaurant** on Moon Muang close to Tha Pahe Gate. Enjoy a fruit shake here as you look out over the moat. You can also enjoy a traditional Khantok dinner served to groups of five or six seated on the floor. Khantok dishes include glutinous rice, Burmese and northern Thai-style curries, spiced minced dishes, Chiang Mai sausage, and crisp pork rind. For more information on these dinners that are complemented by live entertainment, check with your hotel or the tourist office (tel. 222-0222).

Helpful Hint
The Tourism Authority of Thailand has a new office in Chiang Mai at 105/1 Chiang Mai-Lamphun Road, on the east side of the Ping River, two blocks south of the Nawarat Bridge. It's open daily 8:30 a.m. to 4:30 p.m. (Tel. 053-248-604.)

DAY 19: THE NORTH

Explore the northern hill country, meet the surviving members of traditional cultures in the tribal villages, and discover artifacts of ancient kingdoms. From the current trekking capital of Chiang Rai, to the famous Golden Triangle, where the Thai, Burmese, and Laotian borders meet on the Mekong River, the north is a rich, largely unspoiled region. Opium poppies used to be the primary cash crop among the tribes here; although the government outlawed and cracked down on cultivation about 20 years ago, opium-smoking rituals are still part of the guarded indigenous culture.

Suggested Schedule

6:00 a.m.	Rise for early breakfast.
7:00 a.m.	Leave on driving tour of northern Thailand.
5:30 p.m.	Return to Chiang Mai.
7:00 p.m.	Dinner.

Days 16 to 22: Option A

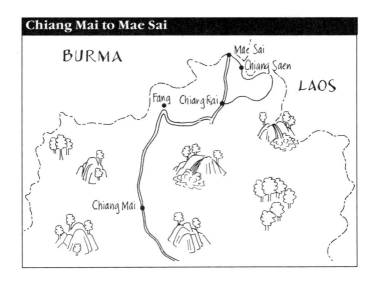

Getting Around
Although you can rent a car in Chiang Mai and attempt to negotiate the roads and traffic yourself, you are better off hiring a driver for a predetermined or personalized tour. For 900 baht ($36) per person, most touring companies will take you on a daylong round-trip to Chiang Rai, Mae Sai, the Golden Triangle, and a hill tribe village. Many options, including elephant riding, waterfall visits, and one-day treks, are available.

Sightseeing Highlights
▲▲▲ **Chiang Rai**—Founded by King Mengrai in 1262, this provincial capital, as yet relatively undisturbed by tourist development, is now a favorite starting point for trekkers. Supposedly founded when Mengrai followed his runaway favorite elephant to the banks of the Kok River, Chiang Rai has two interesting temples—Wat Prasingh, which once housed a significant Theravadan image, and Wat Phra Keo, the original location of the Emerald Buddha.

▲▲▲ **Hill Tribes**—Between 250,000 and 500,000 villagers from various Southeast Asian ethnic minorities still live in tribal settings tucked into the folding foothills of the Himalayas. There are seven major tribes, each with distinctive dress, rituals, and customs. The largest is the Karen, of Tibetan-Burmese stock, many of whom practice an adopted form of Christianity. The Meo, also known as the Hmong, migrated from southern China and were among the most prolific opium poppy growers. The Akha, who came from southern China via Burma, form one of the smallest and poorest tribes, but the women's costuming is among the most intricately sewn and beaded. The Lahu are believed to derive from Tibetan ancestry and still tend toward nomadic ways. The Lawa may be the survivors of original Mon and Khmer peoples. The Lisu are twentieth-century immigrants from southern China, cultivators of opium, and practitioners of animist religions. The Yao migrated from central China, through Laos and Burma, in the early twentieth century. In recent years, development and assistance agencies, such as the government-sponsored Hill Tribe Foundation, have attempted to bring education and health services to the tribes, change cultivation from opium to legal crops, and develop markets for the many tribal handicrafts. Assimilation and "civilization" may be inevitable, but, at present, tribal practices still survive.

▲ **Golden Triangle**—Although there is little more here than a garish sign indicating the location, several handicraft and souvenir stands, and a restaurant, the Golden Triangle is a popular stop on northern tours. The Mekong River reaches out to Burmese and Laotian shores, and longtail boats will take you for fast, exciting rides up and down the smooth-surfaced water. Good, fresh, spicy fish dishes are available at the small restaurant that overlooks the river.

▲▲▲ **Chiang Saen**—Downriver from the Golden Triangle, 37 miles northeast of Chiang Rai, this ancient capital, founded in the thirteenth century, was the center of power for King Mengrai's consolidation of the north. It came under Burmese control in the sixteenth century, was regained by the Chakri dynasty, and later was destroyed by Rama I, who sought to fend off another Burmese invasion. Rama V initiated the city's resurrection, and in 1957 it became a district seat. Among the intriguing historical sights are Wat Pa Sak, a restored chedi from 1295, Wat Phra That Chom Kitti, a tenth-century hilltop chedi, and Wat Chedi Luang, a thirteenth-century chedi rising 186 feet from an octagonal base. You won't want to miss the displays of tribal artifacts at the small museum next door to Wat Chedi Luang.

Itinerary Option: Trekking
Most trek operators offer three- to seven-day treks through the hills around Chiang Mai, Chiang Rai, and the increasingly popular Mae Hong Son region. These tours typically include bus or car transportation to a starting point, hiking through the jungle with local guides, travel on elephantback, and meals and overnight stays with one or more of the hill tribes. To accommodate travelers on tight schedules, some operators have developed one-day "treks" that reveal less of the authentic backcountry way of life but offer a chance to visit a hill tribe, ride an elephant, or take a raft trip.

If you choose to extend your stay in Chiang Mai and explore more of the province, countless tour companies and agencies have set up shop in and around nearly every hotel and guest house. **Mai Ping Leisure Tours**, 95/8 Nimmanhemin Road (opposite the Rincome Hotel), is a professional and friendly operation (tel. 215-126). **Bamboo Tour** (tel. 236-501), **S.T. Tours & Travel** (tel. 212-829), **Ping Tour & Travel** (tel. 236-310), **Meo Tour Services** (tel. 235-116), and **Lamthong Tour** (tel. 235-440) are just a few more of the many trek and tour services available. Many of our readers find that their treks out of Chiang Mai are a highlight of their Asian journey.

DAY 20: CHIANG MAI

This is the day for your closest inspection of Chiang Mai, including its historical temples and its many handicraft workshops, and for taking in the panoramic view of the city from the fantastic mountaintop temple on Doi Suthep. In the evening, stroll through the exciting night bazaar, one of Thailand's best.

Suggested Schedule

9:00 a.m.	Explore temples and shops
12:30 p.m.	Take handicrafts tour.
3:30 p.m.	Visit Doi Suthep.
6:00 p.m.	Dinner.
7:00 p.m.	Stroll through the night bazaar.

Sightseeing Highlights

▲▲▲ **Wat Chiang Man**—Chiang Mai's oldest temple, on Rjaphakinar Road, built in typical Lanna style with Laotian influences, was the residence of King Mengrai while he oversaw the construction of his capital city. It houses the revered Crystal Buddha (Phra Setang Khamani) and a bas-relief stone Buddha (Phra Sila) believed to have come from India after the eighth century.

▲▲▲ **Wat Phra Sing**—this large compound at the corner of Singharat and Rajadamoen roads dates from the reign of King Pha Yu in 1345 and contains a variety of buildings in several styles. The most important is the small, old chapel in which the Phra Singh Buddha image is enshrined. According to legend, the statue originated in Sri Lanka more than 1,500 years ago and was brought to Chiang Mai during the Sukothai period.

▲▲ **Wat Chedi Luang**—A violent earthquake that shook Chiang Mai in 1545 brought down much of the giant, 283-foot-high pagoda here, and the chedi was never repaired. But its enormous base and partial spire, originally constructed in 1401, are still the most significant structures in this Phra Pokklao Road temple area. The

Emerald Buddha was enshrined here at one time. Legend says King Mengrai died close by when struck by lightning. "the spirit of the city" is allegedly safeguarded by the towering gum tree near the wat's entrance.

▲▲ **Handicrafts**—Thanks to the tourist influx, Chiang Mai has northern Thailand's largest concentration of cottage industries. All along the roads to Bor Sang (the "umbrella village") and San Kamphaeng (the center of silk and cotton weaving) are miles and miles of indigenous crafts. Any tuk-tuk or minibus driver will be delighted to take you to buy and witness the making of lacquerware, wood carvings, silverware, jewelry, celadon pottery, umbrellas, and silk. Drivers should charge no more than 120 baht (about $5) per person for a full tour of the handicrafts area.

▲▲▲ **Wat Phrathat**—About 10 miles northwest of town, past Chiang Mai University and a strip of luxury hotels, the land begins a steep rise culminating in a peak over 3,000 feet high. Here sits the dazzling Wat Phrathat, an intricately detailed mountainside temple rife with gilded Buddha images, parasols, and tiled chedis. Two long, colorful dragons snake down as railings alongside the 290 steps that lead to the temple. This vantage point offers a grand view of Chiang Mai and the surrounding hills and plains.

▲▲▲ **Phuping Palace**—Farther up the mountain from Wat Phrathat is the summer palace of King Bhumibol, evidence of royalty's good judgment in choosing a retreat from Bangkok's sweltering heat and pollution. Audience halls, official buildings, guest houses, kitchens, and dining rooms make up the complex, but only the grounds, bursting with bright tropical flowers, are open to the public.

▲▲▲ **Night Bazaar**—Chiang Mai has plenty of markets, such as Warorot for produce (at the corner of Chiang Mai and Wichayan), Suan Buak Hat for flowers (next to the Suan Prung Gate), and Somphet for fruit (at the northeast corner of the moat). But the night bazaar along Chang Khlan Road is the most exciting. Before dusk, hundreds of vendors begin opening their stalls or setting up on the sidewalks. Hill tribe people come into the city to sell their crafts. General merchandise stores entice customers with piles of goods and garish displays. The street is a peaceful riot of buyers and sellers, natives and tourists, music, food, crafts, and trinkets. It gets under way about 6:00 p.m.

DAY 21: KOH SAMUI

You will spend the early part of the day in transit, making airline, bus, and boat connections. But by midday you will be cruising along the typically calm seas off the southeast Thai Peninsula, between the strange shapes and steep cliffs of limestone formations, on a boat full of international travelers. By the late afternoon you will be stretching out on one of southern Thailand's many white sand beaches and wading in the warm, gentle waters of the gulf.

Suggested Schedule

5:30 a.m.	Rise for early departure.
7:30 a.m.	Flight from Chiang Mai to Bangkok.
10:40 a.m.	Flight from Bangkok to Koh Samui.
11:50 a.m.	Arrive at Koh Samui.
1:00 p.m.	Check into bungalow. Relax on beach.

Koh Samui

The largest island in the western Gulf of Thailand, Koh Samui is rapidly becoming popular as an alternative to the touristy coastal resorts at Pattaya ("the Thai Riviera") and Phuket (the large west coast island in the Andaman Sea). It is one of 80 islands in the area, only 4 of which are inhabited. The population of 32,000 was originally sustained by fishing and coconut farming, but as with the entire southern region of Thailand, it is increasingly oriented to tourists and travelers from Japan, Malaysia, and the West. A well-paved road runs approximately 34

Days 16 to 22: Option A

miles around the circumference of the island. Tourist bungalows proliferate, yet it is easy to find an empty expanse of beach. The island interior is largely undeveloped jungle, crisscrossed by rivers that tumble through the hills and cascade down two major waterfalls. Coral reefs off the southern and western coasts provide fine opportunities for snorkeling and scuba diving.

Getting Around

Small pickup trucks, converted into taxis with padded benches and covered beds, congregate at the airport. They charge fixed rates to each of the beach areas, from

15 to 30 baht ($.60-$1.20). Motorbikes (250 baht, or $10, for 24 hours) and jeeps (950 baht, or $38) can be rented in Nathon and at many hotels and bungalows.

Lodging
There is an abundance of accommodations available, everything from the most minimal bungalows with outside plumbing to luxury resorts with doting service and lavish buffets. You might want to ask whether the place you are considering shows videos; a popular attraction is showing movies nightly on videotape, and the action can get noisy.

The most beautiful beach on Koh Samui, Chaweng, naturally has the most hotels and bungalows. The **Imperial Samui**, with more than 70 rooms, lush grounds, and a swimming pool, is one of the island's grand hotels. It charges 1,400 to 2,600 baht ($56-$104) per night for the privilege of a visit (tel. 421-3907) The **PanSea** is close competition in the Club Med mold, offering half-pension and deluxe bungalows for 1,980 to 2,940 baht ($79-$118). The **White House** and the **Village** are much smaller (10 to 20 bungalows) but give the same attention to comfort and more opportunity for privacy at 700 to 1,200 baht ($28-$48). Prices go down as you move to other beaches. On Lamai Beach, the **Pavilion** (350 to 450 baht, or $14-$18) and the **Sand Sea** (500 baht, or $20) are attractive, clean and comfortable. Bo Phut Beach is not as pretty as Chaweng or Lamai (the sand is not as white and the waves are not as dramatic), but, like nearby Mae Nam, it is less crowded and quieter. Here, the **World** bungalows are pleasantly arranged along a garden walk to the beach, and three young women, Tik, Jead, and Yai, offer cheerful service with a wonderful sense of humor. Rates are 600 to 850 baht ($24-$34). Choeng Mon Beach, tucked into a bay on the northeast tip of the island, offers a restful, private getaway at the **P.S. Villa** (50 to 200 baht, or $2-$8) and **Su's Place** (400 to 800 baht, or $16-$32), operated by the same management as the White House and the Village.

Food

Every set of bungalows has its own restaurant, and given the high quality of local cooking, it is virtually impossible to go wrong. Two people can eat well on fresh fruit, seafood, a variety of soups, curries, rice dishes, and desserts for less than 250 baht ($10) per day at the medium-priced accommodations. Eating where you stay also offers the chance to get to know fellow travelers and meet the locals.

DAY 22: KOH SAMUI

The main reason to come to Koh Samui is to stretch out on the sand, beachcomb, and enjoy the clear, warm ocean waters. Today you will take advantage of this idyllic opportunity to wind down at the end of your trip. But you will also spend a few hours taking in some of the manmade sites and natural wonders of the island.

Suggested Schedule

9:00 a.m.	Explore Koh Samui.
Noon	Lunch.
1:00 p.m.	Continue your exploration. Relax, swim, snorkel.

Travel Route

From your hotel or bungalow, rent a motorbike or catch a taxi and ride toward Bo Phut, turning east at the junction that leads to Big Buddha. From Big Buddha, return to the main road, turn left (south), and drive past Chaweng to Lamai Beach. At the southern tip, turn left where the sign directs you to Hin Ta and the Grandmother and Grandfather rocks. From Hin Ta, continue on the main road southwest. Turn right (west) at Baan Hua Thonan, where the road heads inland. Go about one and a half miles and turn right at Baan Thurian onto the dirt road leading to Na Muang Waterfall. Continue north about five and a half miles from Baan Thurian to Baan Lip Yai. Turn right to the

Hin Lad Waterfall. You can either continue your loop around the island or return along the same route.

Sightseeing Highlights

▲▲▲ **Big Buddha**—As you approach Plai Laem Bay at the northeastern tip of Koh Samui, you can see a large figure looming up from Farn Isle, as if rising from the sea. This is Big Buddha, a gigantic seated Buddha image at Hin Nguy Temple. The massive figure dwarfs everything around it, including the other carved figures on the temple grounds and the nearby row of souvenir stands.

▲▲▲ **Grandmother and Grandfather Rocks**—The rocky promontories poking out of Thailand's southern waters assume bizarre and mysterious shapes but none more arresting than the famed Grandmother and Grandfather rocks at Hin Ta. These formations are featured on popular Koh Samui postcards but must be seen to be believed. You reach them by walking down the short path from the paved road turnoff.

▲▲ **Na Muang and Hin Lad Waterfalls**—Most people never leave the beaches on Koh Samui, so the inland jungles are virtually untouched by civilization. The rivers that flow down from the hills tumble into beautiful waterfalls at Na Muang and Hin Lad. These sites were important to early Buddhist inhabitants and are marked by historically significant stone carvings.

Itinerary Options

If you want even more isolation than you find on Koh Samui, the islands of Koh Phangan and Koh Tao are only just beginning to foster tourism. Koh Phangan is about 5 miles due north of Koh Samui, and Koh Tao is another 30 miles northwest. Both are for people who really want to get away from it all and are visited predominantly by backpackers. On Koh Phangan, most of the bungalows are primitive, bare wooden structures built on platforms at the beach, many without electricity or private toilets. If you take the 45-minute boat ride from Nathon to Thong

Days 16 to 22: Option A

Sala, young men and women will recruit you to their bungalows, typically renting for 30 baht ($1.20) per night. Haad Rin, the southern peninsula with the most beautiful beaches, is more developed. Fully equipped bungalows rent here for up to 200 baht ($8). A day trip or overnight excursion to Koh Phangan is possible if you take the 40-minute boat ride from Bo Phut Beach (just past the Oasis) on Koh Samui to Haad Rin. It leaves at 10:00 a.m. and 3:00 p.m. and makes the return trip at 9:00 a.m. and 2:30 p.m. The fare is 75 baht ($3). If Koh Phangan's remoteness and minimal amenities don't appeal to you for an overnight stay, you can make a day trip out of it by catching a boat from Bo Phut Beach (just south of the Oasis bungalows) on Koh Samui to Haad Rin on Koh Phangan. It leaves at 9:30 a.m., arrives an hour and a half later at Chalok Lum, and makes the return trip at 2:30 p.m. The fare is 60 baht ($2.40). Excursions including lunch, for a minimum of four people, are sometimes available for 120 baht ($4.80).

If it's even more isolation you seek, you can continue past Koh Phangan to Koh Tao, a tiny island with breathtakingly clear, sheltered waters for swimming and snorkeling. You can actually swim with sharks in the peaceful bay at Haad Nang Yuan. Bungalows are available on the western and southern beaches. The boat leaving Bo Phut at 9:30 a.m. arrives at Mae Head on Koh Tao at 1:30 p.m. If you are traveling between May and October, when the weather can be unpredictable and schedules are apt to be disrupted, check with a Songserm office before making plans to travel by sea. In Bangkok, call (02) 250-0768, 252-5190, or 252-9654. On Koh Samui, call (077) 421-228, 421-078, or 421-316.

You'll return to Bangkok tomorrow morning, catching the 9:00 a.m. flight from Koh Samui to Bangkok. Turn in early, as your flight back to the U.S. West Coast leaves early the next morning.

DAYS 16 TO 22: OPTION B
BALI

Bali is an island of overwhelming cultural harmony. Although a week is hardly long enough to fully appreciate the geography, the arts, and the people, six or seven days in Bali can affect you in far greater ways than you might imagine. A 2,000-square-mile volcanic island lying eight degrees south of the equator in the Indonesian archipelago, Bali is just a few miles east of Java but stands as a virtual world apart. Most of its 2.5 million inhabitants are Hindu, whereas most of Indonesia is Moslem; their religion, oriented toward the mountains that sweep up from the sea, is a uniquely balanced and taboo-free form of Hinduism. Spiritual concerns are inextricably interwoven with the routines of daily life. Worship—of ancestors and spirits manifested in nature but unified in a single god—is a constant state of mind underlying and shaping material existence. Offerings of woven straw, rice, and flowers are made throughout the day in homes, fields, workshops, and temples. Painting, carving, music, and dance all reflect and extend the harmonious Balinese world view.

Mexican artist Miguel Covarrubias visited Bali in the 1930s and recorded his detailed impressions in *Island of Bali*, still in print and available through KPI publishers. He wrote about the unity of Balinese life and its environment: "Like a continual undersea ballet, the pulse of life in Bali moves with a measured rhythm reminiscent of the sway of marine plants and the flowing motions of octopus and jellyfish under the sweep of a submarine current. There is a similar correlation of the elegant and decorative people with the clear-cut, extravagant vegetation; of their simple and sensitive temperament with the fertile land."

Today, Bali is struggling with the overlay of civilization that was spurred on by Dutch colonialism in the late nineteenth and early twentieth centuries. Over 200,000 people visit Bali annually in a tourist tide that started in the 1930s. Because Bali offers beautiful beaches, warm tropical waters, a terrain of terraced rice fields, coconut palms, and towering volcanoes, plus a fascinating culture, the island has become a vacation ground for Australians, Japanese, and Europeans, as well as a favorite retreat for world travelers on long journeys. Hordes invade the beach resorts of Kuta, Legian, Nusa Dua, and Sanur, attracted to the surfing, the hotels, the nightlife, the shopping, and the beaches. Far fewer stay inland, where the heart and soul of Balinese culture are still vibrantly intact.

The capital city of Denpasar is the center of commerce, with a bustling population of more than 100,000. By far Bali's biggest city, overshadowing Gianyar, Klungkung, and Singaraja, it is crowded and energetic. But out in the villages, which are organized under eight governmental districts corresponding to ancient rajadoms, most people still work in the rice fields or at their crafts. Their social lives revolve around work, temples, and communal economic and fraternal groups. During the Dutch colonization, which ended formally in 1949, the Balinese strongly resisted foreign influence, and as one of 26 provinces of the Republic of Indonesia, founded by Sukarno in 1956, the island still has an independent character. Living under the watchful spirits of the Batur, Agung, and Batuku volcanoes, the Balinese go about their daily lives in deep, calm rhythms that have not been thrown off by the significant new invasion of travelers. They welcome visitors, not only as consumers of arts, crafts, food, and lodging but as honored guests in their homes. Although many villagers speak only native Balinese, most islanders speak Bahasa Indonesian, a relatively easy language to learn. A good phrase book, such as the Lonely Planet *Indonesia Phrasebook*, can provide enough words and grammar for the conscientious visitor to communicate. The Balinese are extraordinarily accommodating.

DAY 16: FROM HONG KONG TO UBUD, BALI

Today you fly to Bali, a highlight of any trip to Asia. Your ride from the airport takes you through the verdant countryside to Ubud, a fascinating village where just about everyone seems to be an artist.

Suggested Schedule

1:00 p.m.	Depart for Hong Kong's Kai Tak Airport.
3:45 p.m.	Fly to Denpasar, Bali.
8:30 p.m.	Arrive in Denpasar.
10:30 p.m.	Arrive in Ubud. Check into your hotel.

Arrival

On arrival at the Denpasar Airport, after clearing immigration and customs, exchange money at one of the bank offices located just outside and to the right of the building exit. The exchange rate, about 1,900 rupiah to the dollar, varies by only a few rupiah from one official moneychanger to the next. For a quick mental conversion from rupiah prices to approximate dollar equivalents, divide by two and move the decimal left three places. For example, 10,000 rupiah equals about $5.

The most reliable transportation from the airport to Ubud can be arranged at the taxi desk, which is situated just outside the airport doors and toward the left end of the building. The prices are fixed, and the 45-minute to one-hour ride to Ubud should cost about 40,000 rupiah ($20). Some independent drivers, waiting outside the airport, will negotiate slightly, but not dramatically, lower rates. Don't rent a car or hire a driver on a long-term basis. Wait until you are in Ubud, where prices are lower. (Tips on car rentals and drivers are given in Days 17 and 18.)

Lodging

Because of the growing influx of tourists, all sorts of accommodations are available in Ubud, from economical *losmen* (homestays) to full-service hotels. The most expensive and most beautiful hotel in Asia is the **Amandari**. It was built in yellow marble to resemble an ancient

Balinese village. Individual cottages are masterpieces of Balinese architecture and modern comfort. If you want the best, ask for Mick Jagger's suite, with a beautiful private swimming pool rimmed by the rice fields. This hotel is located on a ridge overlooking the river on the outskirts of the village of Tjampuhan, a short taxi ride from Ubud. Call in advance to tour the grounds. In the evening, a woman's gamelan orchestra performs beside the most magical swimming pool on the island. Rates start at 440,000 rupiah ($220) a night, but you can tour for nothing. The **Hotel Tjampuhan** (P.O. Box 15, Ubud, Bali; tel. 62 0361-95368; fax 95137) is gorgeously situated on a hillside overlooking a lush river canyon at the western end of town in the neighborhood of Campuhan. Although the rate of 120,000 to 160,000 rupiah ($60-$80 per night), plus tax and service charge, is high by Ubud standards, the bungalows are clean and comfortable, have hot water showers, and are serviced by an attentive, friendly staff. A large breakfast of fruit, pancakes, omelets, toast, and coffee or tea is brought to your room in the morning. The hotel also features Ubud's best swimming pool, especially welcome after a long day of travel.

A few minutes out of town, up the Campuhan Ridge, the **Ananda Cottages** (P.O. Box 205, Denpasar, Bali) offer a variety of attractive rooms and houses in a garden setting surrounded by beautiful rice fields. The atmosphere is quiet, and the restaurant is an especially pleasant spot for a drink or snack. It, too, has a swimming pool. Rates range from 30,000 rupiah ($15) for one room to 120,000 rupiah ($60) for a house. If you prefer to stay in the center of town, the **Hotel Puri Saren**, located on the main road in the middle of Ubud, puts you in the lap of traditional Balinese luxury. It is the home of Prince Corkorda Agung, and the immaculate bungalows, situated in a private garden courtyard and appointed with antiques, reflect his royal taste. The rates, 70,000 rupiah ($35) including breakfast, are at the high end of the Ubud scale. Located up the steps opposite the Tjampuhan

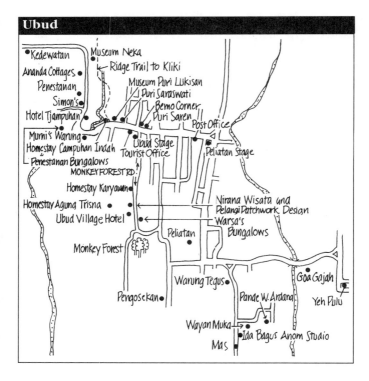

Hotel is the **Penestanan Bungalows.** It offers rooms and bungalows from 34,000 to 40,000 rupiah ($17-$20) including breakfast. There's a good swimming pool and a view of the entire Ubud region. There's a steep climb to reach the Penestanan village plateau, but you'll be in the Bali of 50 years ago and away from the traffic.

Budget housing is available in dozens of modest losmen throughout Ubud. Here you can get a feel for everyday family life and be treated to the essence of Balinese hospitality. The **Homestay Karyawan**, where the sign reads "Accommodation in Beautiful Garden," is located on Monkey Forest Road about a quarter of a mile down from the main road on the right-hand side. It has several large, clean cottages in a neatly landscaped setting surrounded by rice fields and is overseen by an especially friendly hostess who also runs a small shop out front.

Breakfast is included in the 20,000 rupiah (about $10) rate. Another recommended homestay in the Monkey Forest Road area is **Agung Trisna** (behind Putra Silver). It has four rooms. The large double has a window view of the river gorge and costs 15,000 rupiah ($7.50) including breakfast. Also recommended in this area is **Warsa's Bungalows**; very nice rooms with fan and hot water go for 20,000 rupiah ($10).

One of our favorites is the **Homestay Campuhan Indah**, operated by I Gusti Nyoman Darta and his extended family. Located at the western end of the main road, next to Ibu Dewi's warung and behind a wall display of traditional masks, the Campuhan Indah has four minimally appointed, but very clean, rooms. They are set behind the main house, and each has an individual front porch facing a quiet garden stream. The Balinese-style bathrooms, with cold-water showers and manual-flush toilets, are constructed as grottoes behind the rooms. The family is gracious and generous, sharing stories and information, serving tea or coffee, and providing a fine breakfast every morning, all for 12,000 rupiah (about $6) a day for two (tel. 62 0361-95087).

DAY 17: UBUD

Learn about the history of the Indonesian people and their arts, sample Balinese cuisine, and ease into the relaxed pace of life on this charming island famous for its dance performances.

Suggested Schedule	
9:00 a.m.	See Ubud's historical sites and arts and crafts.
Noon	Lunch.
1:00 p.m.	Continue exploring and shopping in Ubud's arts and crafts shops.
6:00 p.m.	Dinner.
7:30 p.m.	Attend dance performance.

Ubud

The capital of Balinese culture, Ubud is a fascinating blend of ancient traditions and gradual modernization. Although it has become a busy, prosperous village catering to tourists on day trips from Bali's beach resorts, Ubud moves with a calm underlying pulse, enticing visitors to settle in for weeks or months at a time.

Driving into Ubud from the countryside between the airport and the village can be disconcerting at first if you are expecting a quaint tropical town of dirt roads and straw huts. There is one main thoroughfare, a straight, paved road extending about a mile from Peliatan on the east end to Campuhan on the west. A second important road, Monkey Forest Road, forms an intersection at the center of town and extends about half a mile south into a real monkey forest. Both roads are lined with shops, studios, and restaurants. On market days—every third day—Ubud gets congested with trucks and bemos. But soon you spy the many temples between the storefronts and see villagers setting out offerings of incense, rice, and flowers. Behind the shops, on the narrow side streets of cloistered residences, activity settles down, and beneath the superficial overlay of commerce, everyday life has an unhurried pace and an almost mystical quality. During the past 50 years, dozens of European and American artists have succumbed to Ubud's lure, establishing permanent homes and developing the vibrant cross-cultural exchange that has guided the village's gradual growth. Arts and crafts are evident in every home, restaurant, temple, and shop.

Surrounded by patches of palm-studded jungle and vast expanses of rice fields in various stages of cultivation, Ubud is the best starting point for an exploration of Bali. The village itself warrants several days of investigation, and from here you can venture out to other points on the island.

Sightseeing Highlights

▲▲▲ **Arts and Crafts Shops**—As soon as you start walking from your hotel, you will begin encountering the myriad arts and crafts of Ubud. Although painting is the local specialty, shop owners gather masks, wood carvings, fabrics, jewelry, baskets, and clothing from all over the region. Shopping here takes on the added dimension of cultural education as you are exposed to an astounding array of handicrafts. Generally, the prices in Ubud are comparable to those in other villages and only slightly higher than in Denpasar and Kuta. But if you are seeking bargains on any particular craft, you should try to go to the source, the village where it is the local specialty: for example, Tampaksiring for earrings (wooden), Pujung for wooden banana trees, Mas for woodcarving, and so forth. Across the street and to the right of the Tjampuhan Hotel, an American named Simon has set up his For Earth Only design shop and gallery, featuring wild and futuristic prints hand silk-screened by local youth. Just down the hill toward town, Murni has added shops selling the latest in Balinese and Indonesian fashions alongside her riverside restaurant. Once into the central section of Ubud, it seems like every other building is a shop of some kind. Here you will find batik, intricately woven ikat fabrics, silver and mother-of-pearl jewelry, and examples of all the other crafts. Browsing is welcome, and bargaining is expected unless a "Fixed Prices" sign is posted. A good starting point for bargaining is half the initial asking price. The shops continue all the way down through Ubud to Peliatan, as well as down Monkey Forest Road. The quality of goods is similar from one place to the next, so don't feel pressured to buy the first things you see. Caveat emptor: there are very few authentic antiques available in these shops, but contemporary craftspeople frequently paint and scuff their pieces to give an antique appearance. From Murni's, turn right (east) and walk up the gradual grade into Ubud. You'll pass under a small aqueduct and come to the beginning of Ubud's main commercial strip. Browse through shops on your way to the Puri Lukisan Museum.

▲▲▲ Puri Lukisan Museum (Palace of Fine Arts)— Located on the left-hand (north) side of the road, the museum's entrance is set back from a small parking area next to the Mumbul Inn and leads to a path that crosses a stream in a spacious garden.

Nearly every village in central Bali is associated with a particular art or craft. Since the 1930s, when German and Dutch painters such as Walter Spies and Rudolf Bonnet settled here and encouraged local artists to develop new styles out of ancient traditions, Ubud (along with nearby Batuan to the south) has been a vital center of Balinese painting. Taking off from the rigid conventions of traditional, narrative *wayang* styles (based on *wayang kulit*, shadow puppet theater), painters began creating individualistic styles. Mythical themes and everyday life in the villages and rice fields are portrayed in meticulous detail. The Puri Lukisan opened in 1956 and has built up a large collection of paintings, sculpture, and wood carvings, from such masters as Gusti Nyoman Lempad of Ubud to members of the contemporary "young artists" movement of nearby communities such as Pengosekan and Penestanan. The galleries are organized to provide a historical survey of the evolution of regional arts. They are open daily from 10:00 a.m. to 4:00 p.m. Admission is 500 rupiah (about $.25).

▲ **Puri Saraswati**—From the museum, turn left and continue east about 100 yards on the main road. On the same side of the street, past the Lotus Café, you will find Ubud's main temple. Every Balinese village has at least three temples: the Pura Pusen, honoring village ancestors; the Pura Desa, for Brahma, where current ceremonies are held; and the Pura Dalem, honoring the dead and the deities of the afterlife. In addition, each family has a small temple in the household compound, and numerous other temples and shrines are placed throughout the community. They are open-air mazes of walls, courtyards, gargoyle-like stone carvings, thatched pavilions, multi-tiered *merus* (towers), platforms, and shelters. Ubud's main temple, located in the center of town near Bemo Corner and next to the lotus pond, is not as spectacular as many others around Bali but is nonetheless a fascinating construction, a calm, introspective place, central to the spiritual life of the villagers. Proper dress—sarongs and sashes for women, long pants or sarongs and sashes for men—is required in all temples.

▲▲**Puri Saren**—After leaving the temple, turn to your left and continue east on the road for about 50 yards. At Bemo Corner, on the northeast side of the intersection, you will see the palace of Ubud's historical royal family. Here you can still meet a real prince, the Cokorda Agung, and catch a glimpse of the opulent life-style enjoyed by the privileged classes of the raja era. Located in the center of Ubud, the palace is a walled complex of neat gardens, handsome bungalows, and ancient stone carvings. Today, the bungalows are rented out to visitors at daily rates starting at 70,000 rupiah (about $35) including breakfast. Turn right down Monkey Forest Road for more shops. Be sure to check out the original children's clothes and quilts at Pelangi Patchwork Design.

▲▲▲**Dance Performances**—On any given night you have a choice of several performances at various stages in and around Ubud. The tourist office, located across the street from the temple, posts schedules of the events with times, locations, and the types of dances. At your hotel, the staff is always aware of what dances are happening each evening. In addition, throughout the day, men sell tickets in the streets of Ubud for the same price as is charged at the door.

The highly stylized dances are staged to entertain and accommodate the curiosity of tourists, but they are founded on religious belief and still retain their spiritual aura. The oldest dances are nearly a thousand years old, deriving from the ancient Gambuh, but most of the popular dances date from the second half of the nineteenth century. Most are performed to the music of the *gamelan*, the delightfully clanging orchestra of drums, cymbals, brass gongs, kettles, and metallophones (a resonant, xylophonelike bronze and bamboo instrument). The rhythmically complex, polyphonic music creates a mesmerizing background for the equally hypnotic dances.

Four of the most frequently performed Balinese dances are the Legong, the Barong, the Kecak, and the Topeng. The Legong, the Heavenly Dance of Divine Nymphs, is performed by elaborately costumed girls, usually 14 years of age or younger. It dramatizes twelfth- and thirteenth-century stories about the King of Lasem and his battles to win the maiden Ragkesari. Its merits hinge on the graceful precision, the unison choreography, and the elegant hand movements of the young dancers.

The Barong dance brings to life a mythical, white magic beast, Barong, who defends the people against the black magic witch, Rangda. Their battle is danced in fantastic costumes and gigantic masks.

The Kecak, or Monkey Dance, takes place in firelight and involves a seated chorus of 150 men who chant and chatter in eerie counterpoint and in unison. Individual dancers act out mythical stories against the background of strange human sounds and swaying movements of the chorus. The best Kecak is performed in the nearby village of Bona.

The Topeng, or Mask Dance, is drawn from centuries of tales about the exploits of noble families and heroes. The masks, often worn in succession by one dancer, are archetypes that magically come to life through the exacting and highly animated movements of the dancer.

If you are in Ubud on a Saturday night, by all means catch a performance of the Peliatan Legong. This troupe dates back to the early twentieth century and was the first company to tour the West. Its young dancers and veteran musicians still represent the height of Balinese culture.

Food

You could spend a month eating your way through Ubud and still not have sampled everything. Several restaurants cater to Western tastes, with prices to match. A full meal might cost between 4,500 and 10,000 rupiah (about $2.25-$5) per person at any of them. **Murni's,** next to the Campuhan River bridge, is one of the most popular spots, serving hamburgers, milk shakes, lasagna, excellent

Days 16 to 22: Option B

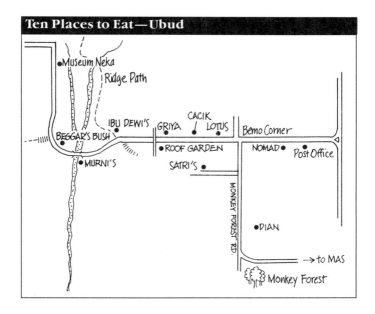

Ten Places to Eat—Ubud

desserts, and coffee, as well as Indonesian dishes. Murni also stocks a fine bookshelf of material about Bali. The **Lotus Café**, in central Ubud, features pasta specials and a lovely view of the immense lotus pond in front of the temple. It is a good place to meet Western travelers. **Beggar's Bush**, on the other side of the bridge from Murni's, serves good steaks and deliciously spiced fish dishes. Upstairs, the coziest late night bar in town plays taped blues and R&B music and closes whenever the last customer leaves.

The more moderately priced restaurants, where you can fill up for $2, also serve more indigenous cuisine. **Griya**, on the main road in Ubud, serves superb tuna *sate, nasi goreng* (fried rice with egg and bits of meat and vegetables), avocado salad, *jaffles* (closed, fried sandwiches), and banana pancakes. **Nomad**, at the eastern end of town, has delicious beef kabobs and *mie goreng* (fried noodles). **Dian**, an extremely inexpensive Javanese restaurant down Monkey Forest Road, serves a wonderful chicken curry and exceptional black rice pudding.

Cacik, not far from Griya, has the cheapest and tastiest *nasi campur* (steamed rice with assorted helpings of chicken, vegetables, tempeh, fish, and other tidbits) and chicken sate. **Satri's**, on Monkey Forest Road behind the Ubud performance stage, is operated by a delightful woman whom many consider the finest cook in Ubud. She makes wonderful tomato soup (prepared for each order), guacamole, mixed fruit *lassis* (yogurt drinks), and special Balinese dinners (about $4.50 per person) organized around your choice of two mouth-watering traditional dishes, banana chicken or smoked duck, either of which should be ordered a day in advance.

Even less expensive snacks and meals are available at any of the small roadside warungs, one- or two-person operations serving a variety of foods from fruit salads and juices to soups and rice dishes. Most serve the same types of foods, prepared with individual flare. **Ibu Dewi**, whose warung is beyond the western end of Ubud on the way to Murni's, makes excellent fruit salads and scrumptious black rice pudding, each for less than $1. The warung next door has delicious banana fritters. **Ibu Putu**'s small warung up the steps across the road from the Hotel Tjampuhan (look for the sign for Rasman's Houses) serves an extraordinary fresh tomato soup, good noodle soups, and fruit drinks.

A host of good restaurants are located along Monkey Forest Road. Moving south from the center of town, try **Gayatri** for sweet and savory waffles. **Lilie**'s has delicious unusual appetizers, wonderful vegetarian nasi campur, an array of tempting desserts, and many dishes you won't find elsewhere. **Cafe Wayan** features shrimp and prawn dishes, Indonesian fare (on a varied menu that includes perhaps the best pizza in town), and especially noteworthy baked goods—breads, cinnamon rolls, pies, and chocolate cake. The **Udit Bakery**, in addition to espresso drinks, offers freshly baked croissants and Danish and French bread. Somewhat out of the way, but made more appealing for its isolated location on the end of Jalan Hanoman in Padang Tegal (southeast Ubud), is the **Dirty Duck Diner,** which has a full menu of rice, noodle, curry, and meat dishes somewhat Westernized but expertly prepared, capped by delicious desserts such as the acclaimed apple crisp. Finally, the newest addition to Ubud nightlife is **Coconut's Cafe,** located about 100 meters north of the main road behind the cinema, which serves a full menu of Indonesian and Western dishes (pizza, pasta, ice cream), has a full bar, and shows a different laser disc movie on a large screen, big sound TV every night.

A few words on Nasi Campur: The most common Indonesian meal is a generous portion of white rice (*nasi putih*) served with small portions of such foods as chicken, fish, egg, coconut, vegetables, tempeh, tofu, and sambal. This individual version of "rice table" is different everywhere, and while the restaurants serve attractive, tidily presented renditions for 1,800 to 3,500 rupiah ($1.90-$1.75), we've found that the best, spiciest, and most authentic Indonesian nasi campur is the cheapest—700 to 1,500 rupiah ($.35-$.75)—served in the smallest warungs. Our two favorites are **Warung Putri Kembar,** a Javanese stand on the east side of the Seni Warna art supply store (east of the post office), and **Warung Tegus,** located about 60 meters south of the Peliatan/Mas junction on the road to Mas. This is real Balinese food.

Helpful Hint

The tourist office usually has walking maps of Ubud and posts the performance schedules of the various Legong, Barong, Kecak, Fire, and other dances in Ubud and neighboring villages.

DAY 18: AROUND UBUD

Today you can step back in time 600 to 900 years and explore two fantastic ruins deeply etched with religious significance. One is a popular site for tourists, and deservedly so; the other, one of Bali's hidden treasures, is rarely visited. A sunrise walk along Campuhan Ridge will steep you in the tranquil rhythms of rural Balinese life. In the afternoon, visit the workshops where some of Bali's finest wood carving is done and see how much time and craft goes into the finished products.

Suggested Schedule

6:00 a.m.	Take a prebreakfast walk along Campuhan Ridge.
8:00 a.m.	Breakfast at hotel.
9:00 a.m.	Bemo to Goa Gajah and Yeh Pulu.
Noon	Lunch in Ubud.
1:00 p.m.	Bemo to the wood carving villages of Mas and Peliatan.
4:30 p.m.	Return to your hotel, make driving arrangements for the next day.
6:30 p.m.	Dinner in Ubud.
7:30 p.m.	Dance performance in Ubud.

Getting Around

For short trips between villages on Bali, bemos (covered trucks with benches for seats) are the economical way to travel. They are not always comfortable. Drivers will load passengers, including Balinese carrying goods to or from market, to the bursting point. Be sure to ask the going rate, as tourists are sometimes charged more than locals. A two- or three-mile trip should cost no more than 200 rupiah (about $.12) per person. The transportation hub of Ubud is Bemo Corner, the village's one main intersection, where Monkey Forest Road meets the main street. Public bemos, which drive along set routes, park here to recruit passengers to various destinations. Privately operated bemos with negotiable fares to the destination of your choice are available for hire here as well.

From Bemo Corner, take a bemo heading east toward Gianyar. Tell the driver you want to stop at Goa Gajah. The road from Ubud turns right at Peliatan, continues for

Days 16 to 22: Option B

one mile, and turns left toward Mas. It is about one mile due east on this road to Goa Gajah. From Goa Gajah, tell the bemo driver you want to stop at Yeh Pulu. Continue east for one-half mile to a major T-junction. Turn right toward Gianyar. About one hundred yards south, the road turns left. Stop here at the sign for Yeh Pulu. The return to Ubud retraces the same route. In the afternoon, you can catch a public bemo to Mas for about 200 rupiah. To return from Mas to Ubud, just stand on the left side of the road and flag down an oncoming bemo.

Sightseeing Highlights
▲▲▲ **Campuhan Ridge**—The early morning hours in Bali are perfect for walking, typically cool and misty, with sunlight filtering down through the palm trees. Rise with the dawn and the crowing of roosters for an invigorating walk along the crest of grassy Campuhan Ridge. You can pick up the trail below the swimming pool at the Hotel Tjampuhan or immediately off the left of the dirt road that passes to the left of the Homestay Campuhan Indah. The hard-beaten dirt path leads north. You will see children walking to school, women carrying baskets of goods on their heads on their way to market, and duck herders guiding their flocks to the rice fields. The ridge leads into great plains of rice paddies in various states of cultivation. About 3 miles north, you encounter the small village of Kliki, where children are likely to be flying homemade kites up and down the dirt roads. At a leisurely pace, you can walk to Kliki and back to Ubud in two hours.

▲▲ **Goa Gajah**—The entrance to the famed Elephant Cave is a phantasmagoria of stone carvings in the shapes of animals, leaves, and grotesque human forms. Goa Gajah dates back to the eleventh century and may have been a Buddhist or Hindu hermitage. It is sometimes crowded with tourists but remains worthy of investigation.

▲▲▲ **Yeh Pulu**—There are thousands of temples and holy places on Bali, but few are as mesmerizing as these infrequently visited ruins of a fourteenth-century hermitage. To get to Yeh Pulu, you have to walk a quarter mile or so from the end of the road, down a narrow path, turning right along the small path that runs through a field and along a river. There are frequently children waiting at the head of the path or an occasional guide who will show you the way. Here you will find an ancient wall frieze carved into the stony face of a cliff. About 7 feet high and 80 feet long, the frieze depicts men, women, deities, and animals in mysterious vignettes. Excavated in 1925, the carvings attract very few visitors, and you are likely to find yourself alone as you contemplate the images of Ganesa, Krishna, and assorted creatures.

▲▲▲ **Mas**—Each village around Ubud has its own special crafts and unique styles. The road east from Ubud passes through Peliatan to Mas, a prosperous village of wood carvers and superb mask makers. Here, Ida Bagus Njana developed a singular style of almost surreal carving in the decades from the 1930s through the 1960s. Have your bemo driver drop you off at one end of the village so you can walk along and peruse the many workshops and storefronts. In the middle of Mas, on the east side of the road, look for the studio of Ida Bagus Anom, a master carver of ceremonial and dance masks who has been featured in a PBS National Geographic special. His work is exquisite, often combining human forms with images from the plant and animal kingdoms. Many Westerners have migrated to Bali to apprentice with him and study mask making and dance. On the street that leads east off the main road (about 20 to 30 meters north of Anom's studio) you will find another exceptional mask carver, I. Wayan Muka, who also follows traditional motifs and invents his own modern variations. Follow the road (Jalan Br. Batan Ancak) as it winds through the village, past a school, until it meets Jalan. Turn right (south) and look for the sign of Pande W. Ardana, a remarkable woodcarver who creates amazing works of art from hibiscus, mahogany, and ebony woods. His work includes marvelous studio pieces based on traditional myths and stories and reasonably priced smaller pieces and production work, all of exceptional quality.

Days 16 to 22: Option B

DAY 19: LAKE BRATAN AND SINGARAJA

The volcanic mountains that separate northern and southern Bali create a fascinating cultural divide. Take a 100-mile round-trip through cool, highland croplands and jungles to the northernmost region of the island, where Dutch colonial rule began in the mid-nineteenth century and influenced the local way of life more strongly than in the south. Along the way you can stop at a marvelous monkey forest, climb through the misty mountain range to a great volcanic lake, and descend again to the coast. The return trip includes a luxurious rest stop at a new resort with one of the most spectacular canyon views on all of Bali.

Suggested Schedule

6:30 p.m.	Breakfast at your hotel or homestay.
7:30 p.m.	Ride to Lake Bratan, with stops at Monkey Forest in Sangeh, Pura Taman Ayun at Mengwi, and the Flower and Farmer's Market of Bukit Mungsu.
Noon	Picnic lunch at botanical garden.
1:00 p.m.	Ride to Singaraja and Lovina Beach.
3:30 p.m.	Return trip to Ubud, stopping at Kupu Kupu Barong en route.
7:00 p.m.	Dinner in Ubud. Make arrangements at Satri's for tomorrow's banana chicken or smoked duck dinner.

Transportation

If you were staying in Bali for more than a week, it would be feasible to rent a car or Jeep for your personal use. But as the road markings can be hard to follow until you are familiar with the island's geography, and as driving in Bali is an art itself, we recommend hiring a driver for day trips. In either case, wait until you are in Ubud to make your arrangements, as the rates are lower there than in Denpasar or any of the beach communities. Azman Sukman rents reliable and superbly maintained Jeeps and vans at Nirana Wisata car rental on Monkey Forest Road (fax 0361-52777). Cars rent for 40,000 rupiah ($20) a day plus insurance. His brother Isanin is available for contracted driving at Homestay Campuhan Indah (tel. 0361-95087). They can arrange to drive you on day trips, as well as to the airport for your departure.

If Azman and Isanin are booked up, they can help you find other drivers. Otherwise drivers at Bemo Corner will charge about 60,000 to 65,000 rupiah ($30-$32.50) per day. Drivers can also be found along Monkey Forest Road. Motorbikes rent for about 7,000 to 9,000 rupiah per day ($3.50-$4.50). Be sure to wear a helmet. Bikes rent for 3,500 rupiah ($1.75) per day. For day trips, make arrangements with your drivers the day before. Make sure they understand the route you want to take. Bring along a good map purchased at the tourist office or at Murni's and point out your planned itinerary.

If you insist on driving yourself, an international driver's license is required for car and motorcycle rentals. Most of Bali's main roads are fairly well paved, but they are narrow and can be a challenge to even the most defensive Western drivers. Traffic moves on the left, sometimes at surprisingly high speeds. Drivers use their horns constantly to signal their approach. Trucks often take up most of the roadway, motorbikes zip around everywhere, and some side roads are chockfull of potholes. Foreigners are often assumed liable even in accidents that may not be their fault. We do not recommend driving at night under any circumstances. In fact, why not just do yourself a favor and hire a driver.

Sightseeing Highlights

▲▲▲ **Sangeh**—Here you can experience one of Bali's most intense encounters with wildlife. Hundreds of friendly, pestering monkeys follow you through the forest and temple at Sangeh, begging for the peanuts you can purchase at the entrance. They climb up your leg and perch on your shoulder, taking the nuts from your outstretched hand with their soft fingers. The mythical origins of this Bukit Sari, or Monkey Forest, lie in the legend of Hanuman, the heroic monkey. Part of his monkey army landed here when a section of the holy mountain, Mahameru, fell to earth. The temple, Pura Bukit Sari, was built in the seventeenth century, and its grounds now include a row of booths selling handicrafts. Young, smiling guides are available to keep the monkeys at bay or to help you feed them as you stroll through the forest of nutmeg trees. Beware: remove all money and valuables from your arms, neck, and clothing. The monkeys are notoriously swift pickpockets.

▲▲▲ **Bukit Mungsu**—This large outdoor market presents an eye-popping array of colorful fruits and vegetables of every variety. Women walk through the parking lot selling freshly cooked corn on the cob from the giant pans they carry on their heads. Behind the front stalls of neatly arranged produce is a row of plant and flower stands where vendors sell potted and freshly cut flowers. Dazzling varieties of orchids are the specialties. Lush nurseries extend back from the stalls. Select an assortment of fruits and vegetables for a picnic lunch to take back 2 miles west to the botanical garden or just down the hill ahead to Lake Bratan.

▲▲ **Lila Graha Botanical Garden**—Beyond a spectacular split gate, its ornateness typical of northern carving, acres of trimly cultivated gardens roll gently into the dense woods that cover the nearby hills. This vast forest expanse, visited by relatively few tourists, is dotted with special flower beds and greenhouses. Brilliant arrays of mountain orchids are a major attraction. The garden provides a tranquil setting for a picnic lunch.

▲▲▲ **Lake Bratan**—Filling an ancient crater of the volcanic Mt. Bratan, this large lake provides a surprising alpine vista above the jungle line. The sometimes sun-drenched, sometimes mist-shrouded lake, surrounded by dark forest-covered mountains, is used for fishing, canoeing, and waterskiing. The Ulu Danu Temple, honoring the goddess of the lake, is located on the western shore. There is a small guest house and restaurant on the southern side. After crossing the 1,220-meter mountain pass at Bratan, you will pass the world-class Bali Handara Golf Course and descend into the region of Buleleng heading for Singaraja.

▲▲ **Singaraja**—Founded in 1604 by the Raja Panji Sakti, this cosmopolitan seaport became the Dutch capital at the end of the nineteenth century. Its ethnically diverse population of 25,000 reflects the various waves of immigrants that populated the city, including Chinese, Europeans, Javanese, and the Bugis of Sulawesi. The town is quiet. Its main cultural institution is the Gedong Kirtya, a historical library of Balinese manuscripts, located on Jalan Veteran. The Hindu temples around Singaraja, at Jagaraga, Sangsit, Sawan, and Kubutambahan, reveal the differences between northern and southern styles. Here the carvings are even more ornate and fantastic, some incorporating scenes from everyday life—cars, bicycles, lovers—alongside wild mythical creatures.

▲▲ **Lovina Beach**—Seven miles to the west of Singaraja, you will find this quiet and uncrowded beach resort. The waves are usually gentle, and while the beach is not spectacular, the snorkeling is very good in the clear waters. A refreshing dip in the sea is just the thing to perk you up for the drive back to Ubud. Celuk Agung Beach Cottages in Lovina offers new rooms, fans or air conditioning, a nice pool, and a good open-air restaurant with fresh fish. You'll pay about $25. Other possibilities include Krisna Beach Cottages, Ganeca, and Aditya Hotel. There's good fresh fish at Khi-Khi.

▲▲▲ **Kupu Kupu Barong**—The perfect place to stop at the end of the long drive down from Batur is this luxurious new resort tucked into the hills at Kedewatan, about 3 miles northwest of Ubud. Although its bungalows were expensive and its restaurant was only mediocre the last time we visited, Kupu Kupu Barong boasts one of the most spectacular views on Bali. The Ayung River has cut a deep, winding canyon through the hills, and rice farmers

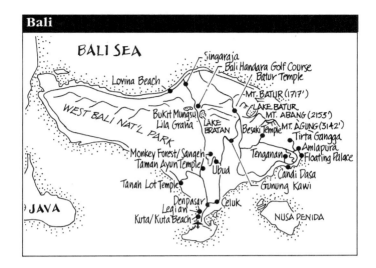

have terraced the land up from the water, creating a complex, multihued relief of blue water, green and yellow paddies, and tangled, palm-studded jungle. Grab a window table in the beautiful restaurant, perched high above the river, and enjoy a cool drink as the sunset transforms the landscape into a magical pink and orange vista.

DAY 20: TANAH LOT

The Balinese most typically look to the mountains for spiritual sustenance, but today you will discover what goes on by the sea. All over the island, the Balinese live in harmony with their environment. Here on the shoreline, they have built a magnificent temple that blends gracefully into the rocky silhouettes of the coast. The drive to Tanah Lot takes you through the main region of Bali's gold and silver production and to yet another spectacular temple. At the other end of the cultural spectrum, in Kuta you can witness what becomes of a sleepy beach area when tourists and entrepreneurs join hands across the pocketbook.

Suggested Schedule

8:00 a.m.	Breakfast at your hotel or homestay.
9:00 a.m.	Bemo to Celuk.
Noon	Lunch in Denpasar.
1:00 p.m.	Bemo to Tanah Lot.
4:00 p.m.	Bemo to Ubud. Arrange for tomorrow's transportation.
7:00 p.m.	Special Balinese dinner at Satri's.

Sightseeing Highlights

▲▲ **Celuk**—About halfway from Ubud to Denpasar, between the villages of Batuan to the north and Batubulan to the south, lies the center of gold and silver crafts in Bali. Along both sides of the main road, workshops and storefronts sell handcrafted jewelry. Prices are usually fixed, but you will find countless bargains on earrings, necklaces, and bracelets in fascinating original designs.

▲▲▲ **Pura Taman Ayun**—Located at Mengwi, the former focus of a mighty kingdom, this unusual temple was built in 1634 and restored three hundred years later in the 1930s. Its multitiered shrines are organized on a wide plateau that rises from a surrounding moat. A large pond in front, a carefully groomed grassy courtyard, and the accompanying gardens make the temple a pleasing pastoral refuge. The altars and pavilions are decorated with intricate wood and stone carvings.

▲▲▲ **Tanah Lot**—Located on the coast due west of Denpasar, about 18 miles on the main road that loops north and then down to the coast, this sixteenth-century temple is built on a huge rock in the shallow waters of the sea. Under the guidance of the priest Nirartha, the people of the local fishing village built the temple to honor the spirits of the sea. One of the most popular postcard vistas of Bali, the temple and rock create ethereal patterns at sunset. You can sit on the beach and watch the shapes and shadows merge into the enfolding dusk.

Food

Denpasar offers a wide variety of luncheon options, from Western staples (including Kentucky Fried Chicken and

Pizza Hut) to Indian and Chinese specialties. But the best choices are native Indonesian, and one of the best cooks can be found at **Bundo Kanduang**, a small, inexpensive restaurant at Jalan Diponegoro 112A. The owner is Javanese, and many of the dishes derive from spicy East Sumatran cuisine. Featured items include *rendang* (meat simmered in spices for 24 hours), *perkedel* (fried, spicy mashed potatoes), and *sambal goreng udang* (shrimps, potatoes, and chilis). You can try them all in a nasi campur for less than two dollars.

Itinerary Option: Kuta and Legian

Less than 30 years ago, Kuta was a quiet coastal village, home to fishermen and metalworkers. Now this bustling beach town, which merges inseparably into Legian at the northern end, is bursting with activity, from the nonstop bartering that goes on in the hundreds of boutiques to the busy beach scenes of surfing and sunbathing. The streets are narrow and frenetic; the shops are small and jam-packed; the restaurants sell pizza, hamburgers, and Mexican food, as well as Indonesian dishes; the beach is full of people insistently hawking everything from sarongs to massages. Compared to the inland villages, rice fields, and temples, Kuta is the "future shock" of Bali. In an hour or two of browsing the shops, you can find almost unbelievable shopping bargains, especially hand-tailored clothes of native fabrics and leathers. Made's Warung, on Jalan Pantai Kuta, is a popular gathering spot for locals and Westerners. Warung Kopi in Legian on Main Street (Legian St.) has a fine bakery for desserts but is especially recommended for several spicy Indian dishes—choice of curry styles—and Middle Eastern foods in a cool back garden terrace setting away from the madding crowd of tourists and shoppers on the street

DAY 21: GUNUNG KAWI, BATUR, AND BESAKI

Today, visit the heart of Bali's spirit world. The second main route into northern Bali takes you to a breathtaking overlook of the island's largest lake, through the foothills of its highest peak, and to the temple that is the "mother" of Bali's religious life. Along the way, you will visit one of Bali's most unusual temples. The daylong, 110-mile trip ends with a refreshing swim in the soothing waters off Bali's finest southeastern beach.

Suggested Schedule

7:00 a.m.	Breakfast at your hotel or homestay.
8:00 a.m.	Check out. Drive to Gunung Kawi, Batur overlook, and Besaki.
12:30 p.m.	Lunch at the warung at Besaki entrance.
1:30 p.m.	Tour Besaki.
2:30 p.m.	Drive to Candi Dasa.
4:30 p.m.	Check into homestay or hotel. Late afternoon swim in ocean.

Sightseeing Highlights

▲▲▲ **Gunung Kawi**—Some 300 steps lead down the steep hillside into the valley of the Pakrisan River, where, according to myth, the giant Kebo Iwa used his fingernail to carve this magnificent "Rocky Temple" out of the side of the mountain in the eleventh century. The enormous *candis* (monuments) are sculpted into deep, arching niches, more than 20 feet high. Five are located on one side of the small Pakrisan River, four on the other. A tenth stands alone at the southern end of the narrow valley. A set of monks' cells is also carved from the stony canyon walls.

▲▲▲ **Lake Batur**—Resting in a broad, 12.5-mile-wide caldera between Mount Batur and Mount Abang, Lake Batur offers one of the most dramatic views on Bali. From the overlook on the road at Penelokan, you stand high above the huge lake, with the slopes of both mountains sweeping down from misty peaks to the silvery reflecting surface of water. The vast lava flows from the devastating eruptions of 1917 and 1926 are easily visible. A narrow road winds down to Kedisan on the shore. Across Lake Kedisan lies Tunyan, one of the last original Balinese villages, where the inhabitants still live according to such ancient traditions as allowing the dead to disintegrate in the open air.

▲▲▲ **Pura Besakih**—The "mother temple" of Bali, also known as Pura Panataran Agung, is situated on the eastern slope of towering Mt. Agung, an active volcano that last erupted in 1963. A complex of more than 30 temples, Besakih has been developed over the course of a thousand years and represents the highest spiritual unity of the entire island. During festival periods, thousands of Balinese make pilgrimages to the temple, the site of holy purification ceremonies. Before making the dramatic ascent to the temple, you can stop for an inexpensive lunch of nasi campur at one of the warungs that line the parking lot. Then walk up the hill through the split gate and tour the terraced towers and shrines of Pura Panataran Agung, often festooned with bright, colorful banners.

Candi Dasa

Developed specifically as a tourist area, Candi Dasa is a strip of hotels, losmen, and restaurants along a narrow beach of soft white sand. Unfortunately, the main beach at Candi Dasa has virtually eroded away, despite the installation of huge T-shaped concrete piers. But the swimming remains good. The atmosphere here is very casual and relaxed. It attracts a crowd of young Australian, European, and American travelers; despite the contrary wishes of the local population, foreign women often sunbathe topless along the beach. Fishermen with outriggers will offer to take you for rides to the giant rocks off the southern end of the beach for excellent snorkeling. Every restaurant has a beachside patio just above the waves. Candi Dasa is a perfect place to wind down after a long day trip.

Lodging

In Candi Dasa, the **Watergarden** at P.O. Box 39, Amlapura, Bali (tel.0361-35540), runs $55 to $60, not including breakfast. It has beautiful bungalows with teak decks on lotus ponds and a fantastic swimming pool with waterfall. The **Sunset Bungalows** at the north end of Balina Beach is the least expensive and most Balinese of the accommodations in this area. Bungalows run 28,500 rupiah ($15) a night for a thatched hut a few steps from the beach.

The **Puri Pandan** and the **Pondok Bamboo**, under one ownership, offer clean, pleasant bamboo cottages along lush garden walks just a few yards from the beach. Rates, from 25,000 rupiah ($12.50) per night, include breakfast. Our favorite place is **Kelapa Mas Homestay** located on the eastern end of Candi Dasa. It has large comfortable cottages facing the beach for about 15,000 rupiah ($7.50) per night. There are also units in the banana tree and coconut palm garden. The whole place offers a feeling of privacy, good breakfasts, and, if you'd like, a massage. P.C. Box 23, Candi Dasa, Karangesm, Bali.

Food

The best beach restaurant in Candi Dasa is **Puri Pandan**. It serves *cumi cumi goreng saus Lombok* (fried calamari in tomato sauce!), grilled fish, lobster, Indian dishes, and fruit drinks. Also recommended on the waterfront is **Pondok Bamboo**. A full dinner costs 5,000 rupiah ($2.50). Another possibility is **Molly's Garden Café.** A big menu includes assorted appetizers (tempeh, hummus), salads, good pasta, many meat and fish dishes, full breakfasts, vegetarian food, and desserts served in an elegant setting. Our favorite Balinese nasi campur is at **Warung Rasmini**, across the street and a few steps east from Kelapa Mas Homestay. Ask for fried fish pedas. Only about 1,100 rupiah ($.55).

DAY 22: CANDI DASA

This is a day to rest, recuperate from your busy schedule of touring, and relish the pleasures of the sea. In contrast to the crazy commerce and nightlife of the Kuta and Sanur beach areas, Candi Dasa remains relaxed and hassle-free. The southeastern coast of Bali has numerous sites for scuba diving, snorkeling, and swimming in warm, crystal-clear waters.

Suggested Schedule

8:00 a.m.	Breakfast at your hotel or homestay.
9:30 a.m.	Scuba diving or snorkeling trip from Balina Beach.
1:00 p.m.	Lunch in Candi Dasa.
2:00 p.m.	Relax on beach. Scuba dive or snorkel.

Scuba Diving and Snorkeling

At the Balina Beach Hotel, a good scuba diving operation supplies equipment, air, transportation, and dive guides for seven different dive spots around the southeastern and northern coast of Bali. Prime locations include the coral gardens around Kambing Island, the "Blue Lagoon," Nusa Penida Island, Amed, Padang Bai, and a sunken U.S. Liberty Ship from World War II at Tulamben. Guides can also arrange to take you on a special night dive at the shipwreck. The comfortable temperatures and marvelous visibility of the Indonesian waters and the abundant undersea life—immense rainbows of hard and soft coral, hundreds of species of exotic fish—make underwater exploration a must, even if you only paddle along on the surface gazing through a mask at the world below. Other operators are Barracuda Bali Dive and Diving School, P.O. Box 1116 (tel. 35536) at Candi Dasa Beach Bungalow II, and Stingray Diving Center, P.O. Box 117, Denpasar. Prices range from $25 to $60 for scuba trips, $5 to $20 for snorkeling.

EXTRA-DAY OPTION: TENGANAN, AMLAPURA, UJUNG, AND TIRTA GANGGA

A perfect way to wind up your visit to Bali is a visit to the unspoiled southeastern regions of the island, where the landscape of low mountains, terraced rice fields, and jagged coastline has been scarred only by volcanic action. The easiest place to arrange for daily transportation is at your homestay or at the Balina Beach Hotel. If you are staying in Candi Dasa, you can catch a public bemo heading west and be dropped off at the hotel's driveway. The parking lot is a regular gathering spot for drivers. You can also make arrangements at the hotel desk. Expect to pay 40,000 to 50,000 rupiah ($20-$25) for an all-day trip.

Sightseeing Highlights

▲▲▲ **Tenganan**—Very few villages of the Bali Aga, the original Balinese, have endured into the late twentieth century. Only 3 miles north of Candi Dasa, Tenganan is one of the last outposts of this old culture. Protected as much by a strong sense of custom, a tradition of communal landownership, and a rigidly maintained isolationism as by the thick wall that surrounds the village, Tenganan is the home of double ikat weaving, the ancient Redjang dance, and an annual festival, Usaba Sambah. The weaving brings Tenganan its greatest notoriety in the modern age. It is a fastidiously intricate process using patterned threads on both the warp and the weft, resulting in the rare "flaming" cloth of dazzling patterns and intense colors.

▲▲▲ **Amlapura**—Formerly known as Karangasem, this village was the center of the Karangasem kingdom, the most powerful regency of late eighteenth- and early nineteenth-century Bali. At the turn of the twentieth century, the raja cooperated with the Dutch colonialists and survived with a modicum of power. The strangely eclectic palace, the Puri Kanginan, combines European, Chinese, and Balinese styles. The last king, Anak Agung Anglurah Ketut, spent much of his late life building water palaces for his royal retreats.

▲▲▲ **Ujung**—The Karangasem king's first palatial construction, the famous Floating Palace, was completed in 1921. Severely damaged by a great earthquake and the devastating eruption of Mt. Agung in 1963, the arrangement of pools, pavilions, moats, and royal bungalow stands in ruins on the beach 5 miles south of Amlapura, a fascinating monument to the king's fantasies.

▲▲▲ **Tirta Gangga**—In 1946, the king undertook a second water palace 9 miles north of Amlapura. It was a series of connected pools shaded by a giant banyan tree. The king and his family could relax in the royal bathing pools and enjoy the view of mighty Mt. Agung above the rolling hills. When the temperamental volcano blew its top in 1963, the elaborate compound and exotic statuary were damaged, but it is still possible to appreciate the pastoral setting and sense of escape that brought the king to this site.

DEPARTURE

You can return to Los Angeles the following day on a direct flight leaving Denpasar in the midafternoon. The food at the Denpasar Airport is mediocre and dreadfully overpriced, and flights are often delayed an hour or more, so it is wise to stop at a warung on the way to the airport and pick up lunch to take with you. The Depot Barito, on Jalan Raya Puputan Nitimandala across from the Department of Justice on the outskirts of Denpasar, is operated by the same family that runs the Bundo Kanduang in Denpasar. You might take a bag lunch of rendang, perkedel, sambal goreng udang, and other Sumatran and Javanese delicacies. Savor them as your plane makes its way back across the Pacific.

Stopover Option: Yogyakarta

Yogyakarta is the spiritual and cultural capital of Java, located in the broad, central plain that spreads out below Mt. Merapi. Usually called "Yogya," it is a busy metropolis of 500,000, teeming with bemos and *becaks* (three-wheeled taxi carts) and dotted with batik galleries, silver workshops, leather factories, wayan kulit (shadow puppet) theaters, and gamelan stages. During a three-day side trip, you can explore the historic sites of the sprawling city, the nearby ancient temples of Prambanan and Borobudur and the quieter twin court city of Solo (Surakarta).

Garuda Indonesian has several flights daily between Denpasar and Yogyakarta. Upon your arrival, be sure to walk across the street from the airport and visit the gallery of Sapto Hudoyo. The dashing, white-haired artist is like the Gucci of Java, a renowned batik designer and a collector of Indonesian artifacts. His gallery is actually a splendid home, organized into showrooms and a spectacular museum.

In Yogya, visit the royal Kraton, the 200-year-old palace at the heart of the city, the dazzling Taman Sari (royal pleasure gardens), and the fascinating bird market. In the surrounding area, visit the ancient temple complex of Borobudur (26 miles northwest of Yogya), which includes the world's largest Buddhist monument; Prambanan, a Hindu temple complex featuring some of Java's most spectacular temples (17 miles east of Yogya); and Solo (38 miles east of Yogya), which offers a chance to appreciate the fine arts and crafts of central Java in a less frenetic setting than bustling Yogya.

Accommodations in Yogya range from the first-class Ambarrukmo Hotel, about $75 a night (Jalan Adisucipto, tel. 8848-8), and the historic Hotel Garuda, about $50 a night (Jalan Marlioboro 72, tel. 2113-4), to budget losmen along the railroad tracks. We recommend the centrally located, midrange guest houses along Jalan Prawirotaman, such as the Duta Guest House at about $15 a night (Jalan Prawirotaman 20, tel. 5219). The Duta, the Metro, and others offer free transportation from the airport and organize excursions to Prambanan and Borobudur.

POSTTOUR OPTION
HAWAII

We've tried all the recommended jet lag remedies for an Asian trip, and we believe none can compare with Hawaii. A favorite of trans-Pacific pilots, this stopover is the best way we know to get back in sync with the American clock. The islands offer a chance to rest, swim, lie on a beach, and enjoy some more Thai food. The extra $50 to $75 for a Hawaii stopover (it may be free if you stop for less than 12 hours) is money well spent.

Even if you only have enough time to hit the beach between planes, we recommend you try our anti-jet lag Hawaii stopover. If you're coming back from Bali on Garuda, the plane goes direct to Hawaii, and there's no extra charge for stopping over here. The only catch is that the Garuda service operates only three times a week, meaning that you'll have to wait at least two days for the next flight. That, of course, is not such a tragedy, given Hawaii's many attractive possibilities. If you're coming back from Bangkok, United and Northwest serve Hawaii via Tokyo. Since they offer daily flights from Honolulu to the states, you'll have more flexibility in your stopover arrangements.

Getting There

After clearing customs, you'll want to rent a car if you plan more than a brief stopover. In addition to the familiar national firms with booths in the airport, a good local company is Tropical Rent-A-Car. The phone number is (808) 957-0800. Your hotel may provide courtesy pickup, or you can take a taxi into Waikiki for about $25. TheBus can also take you to the Ala Moana Shopping Center Terminal for just $.60. Unfortunately, you'll only be allowed to bring along a single carryon bag. To use this service, you'll have to check most of your luggage at the airport. From the Ala Moana Terminal, you'll be able to catch buses to all of the major destinations we recommend during your stay.

A Brief Stay

If you have a limited amount of time and just want to kick back, simply head over to Ala Moana Beach Park, across the way from the bus terminal. About half an hour from the airport, it's located before the Waikiki resorts, meaning you don't have to worry about fighting your way through sometimes heavy traffic. Another plus is that even when the surf is up, a reef ensures safe swimming. Popular with the locals, the lawns adjacent to the beach create a picturesque backdrop to the beach scene. Here you'll be able to buy snacks such as shave ice in your choice of wonderful flavors. Shower at the bathhouse before returning to the airport and your flight home.

A Full Day

If your time is limited but you want to see a little more of Oahu, why not book an evening flight home? This will give you an entire day to sample the best of Honolulu. An excellent alternative to Ala Moana Beach Park is Hanauma Bay. Because of the popularity of this snorkeling spot near Diamond Head, we recommend proceeding here immediately after your arrival. While the snorkeling is not any better than what you may have just enjoyed in Asia, the setting is terrific. If you're visiting on a weekend, head up the Windward Coast to Bellows Field Beach Park (you'll need a car to reach this spot). Part of an air force station, it's open from noon Fridays to midnight Sundays and on federal holidays. A great spot for swimming and bodysurfing, this is a popular choice with the locals. A wooded picnic area provides relief from the hot sun. Standing on the shore, gazing up at the Koolau Range, you may conclude you've found the most beautiful beach in Hawaii.

A perfect place for lunch near downtown is the Garden Café on the patio of the Honolulu Academy of Arts. This outdoor courtyard, staffed by volunteers, is open Tuesday through Friday with seating at 11:30 a.m. and 1:00 p.m. It's located at 900 S. Beretania Street. Call (808) 531-8865. The nearby Mission Houses Museum at 553 S. King Street tells the story of the New England Congregationalists who arrived here in the early nineteenth century to convert the Hawaiians. Touring the modest white frame homes where these pioneering families lived, you'll learn of their struggle to bring the word of God to a native population that had no written language. The museum is open daily from 9:00 a.m. to 4:00 p.m. (tel. 808-531-0481). The nearby Iolani Palace at King and Richard streets is also well worth a visit. Built by King David Kalakaua in 1879, this Florentine landmark was a kind of last hurrah for the Hawaiian monarchy that fell in 1893. Guided tours are offered Wednesday through Saturday 9:00 a.m. to 2:15 p.m. except holidays. Reservations are required; call 538-1471. Another excellent possibility is a visit to the Bishop Museum at 1525 Bernice. The Smithsonian of Hawaiiana and Polynesian culture, this collection provides a splendid introduction to the islands. From artifacts of Hawaiian royalty to celestial navigation in the South Seas, this is an ideal choice for your stopover. Take TheBus #2 to Kapalama Street and walk a couple of blocks west to Bernice Street. Then turn right to the museum. Phone (808) 847-3511.

An Overnight Stay
An overnight visit will give you a chance to see a number of other Oahu highlights, such as the Arizona Memorial commemorating the USS *Arizona*, a ship sunk by the Japanese in their Pearl Harbor raid, taking the lives of the more than 1,100 aboard. The museum here documents the story of this infamous raid with murals, exhibits, and documentary footage. Reached via TheBus #50.

Another excellent choice is the Polynesian Cultural Center on the Windward Coast. Seven villages re-create the traditional cultures of Hawaii, French Polynesia, Fiji, Tonga, and New Zealand. Here you can tour traditional homes, see dance performances and craft demonstrations, and sample local cuisine. This is a great introduction to Pacific island culture, authentically documented by dedicated anthropologists, archaeologists, and historians.

Food

Of the many fine Honolulu restaurants, we recommend three. **The Willows,** at 901 Hausten, is a longtime favorite that provides a fine introduction to Hawaiian cuisine, or if you prefer, Chinese dishes, lamb, and duck are also on the menu. Located in a parklike setting with thatched pavilions and carp ponds, this restaurant also offers entertainment. Call (808) 946-4808. Another good bet is **Keo's** at 625 Kapahulu Avenue. After a visit to Thailand, you may be surprised to learn that one of the world's great Thai restaurants is located right here in Honolulu. Phone (808) 737-8240. Finally, for dinner, a drink, or both, you can't beat the setting at the **Hau Tree Lanai**, located in the New Otani Kaimana Beach Hotel at 2863 Kalakaua Avenue (tel. 808-923-1555). Another good spot for a drink is the oceanfront bar at the **Sheraton Royal Hawaiian**, 2259 Kalakaua Avenue (tel. 808-923-7311). The city's top hula performance is staged by the **Brothers Cazimero**. Tuesday through Saturday you can enjoy the 7:00 p.m. dinner show for $63 or the 9:00 p.m. cocktail show at $19.50. There's also a $30 cocktail show at 10:30 p.m. on Friday and Saturday.

Lodging

The **Waikiki Joy**, 320 Lewers, is an excellent boutique hotel with luxurious oversized rooms and kitchenettes, (tel. 808-923-2300). Rates start at $125. The **Waikikian At The Beach** is that rarest of commodities on Waikiki, a two-story hotel with units built around a tropical garden. At $90, this conveniently located hotel is fine as long as you insist on the low-rise Polynesian-style units. The Tahitian Lanai restaurant here is a local favorite at 1811 Ala Moana Boulevard (tel. 808-949-5331). The previously mentioned **New Otani**, 2863 Kalakaua, with rooms starting around $110 (tel. 808-923-1555), and the nearby **Colony Surf Hotel** at 2895 Kalakaua Avenue (tel. 808-923-5751) are also recommended. Located on Kapiolani Park, these hotels are far enough away from the Waikiki crush to give you the peace and quiet you deserve.

INDEX

Airfares, 5, 6; connecting flights, 5, 6; consolidators, 6; intra-China, 6; nonstop charge, 6; stopovers, 5, 159; Thailand domestic, 6; trip cancellation insurance, 6, 15. *See also* Airlines; Itinerary; Trip

Airlines, 5, 6, 7; additional stops, 5, 6; booking, 7; carrier combinations, 6; nonstop, 6, 7; reservations, 7; scheduling, 7; wholesalers (consolidators), 6. *See also* Airfares; Itinerary; Trip

Amlapura, 156

Badaling (China), 53, 54

Bali, 5, 8, 10; arrival, 130; arts and crafts, 5, 134-136, 144; dance performances, 137-138; description and history, 128-129; exchange rate, 8, 130; food, 9, 138-141, 150-151; getting around, 142-143, 145-146; guidebooks, 13; lodging, 130-133, 153-154; northern, 145, 146-149; public transportation, 10, 142; shopping, 135, 144, 150, 151; sights, 143-144, 146-149, 150, 152-153, 156-157; southeast, 155-157; tourist information, 14. *See also* Candi Dasa; Denpasar; Ubud

Bangkok: description and history, 100-102; exchange rate, 8, 102; food, 106-108; getting around, 102-103, 109-110; lodging, 105-106; nightlife, 108-109; sex industry, 108; sights, 103-105. *See also* Thailand

Beaches, 90, 122, 125, 127, 148, 151, 153, 155, 160

becak (tax cart, Yogyakarta), 157

Beijing: arrival, 44, 46; exchange rate, 8, 46; food, 49; getting around, 52, 56; lodging, 47-49; nightlife, 55; shopping, 50-51; sights, 52-55, 56-59. *See also* China

bemos (public vans, Bali), 10

bento (box lunch, Kyoto), 24

Big Buddha, 126

Bonham Strand East (Hong Kong), 85

Books, recommended, 12-14

Bukit Mungsu (Bali), 147

Bund, the (Shanghai), 3, 65, 66-67

bunraku (classical puppetry, Kyoto), 37

Campuhan Ridge (Ubud), 143

Cancellation insurance, 15

Candi Dasa, 153; food, 154; lodging, 153-154; scuba diving and snorkeling, 155. *See also* Bali

candis (monuments, Bali), 152

Chiang Mai: description and history, 112; food, 115-116; getting around, 113; hill tribes, 116, 118; lodging, 114-115; sights, 117-119, 120-122. *See also* Bangkok; Thailand

Chiang Rai, 117

Chiang Saen, 118-119

Climate in countries, 10

China, 4, 7, 10; arts and crafts, 46, 54, 55, 68, 70, 72; description and history, 44-46; exchange rate, 8, 46; guidebooks, 13; public transportation, 9, 69; tourist information, 14. *See also* Beijing; Shanghai; Suzhou
Cloth Alley (Hong Kong), 84
Clothing, what to take, 12
Consumer Reports Travel Letter, 6
Credit cards, 7
Cultural Revolution, 45, 64

Denpasar, 129; arrival, 130; exchange rate, 8, 130; food, 150-151; leaving, 157. *See also* Bali; Ubud
depaato (department store, Kyoto), 25
Diseases, protection against, 11
Driving, 14, 146

Exchange rates, 7-8. *See also* individual countries

Flights. *See* Airfares; Airlines
Floating Market (Bangkok), 111
Food, 9. *See also* individual destinations
Food precautions, 11
Forbidden City (Beijing), 56-57

gado gado (hot vegetable salad, Bali), 9
gamelan (orchestra, Bali), 137
Golden Triangle, 116
Grandmother and Grandfather Rocks, 126
Grand Palace (Bangkok), 103-104
Great Wall, 52-54
Gunung Kawi, 152
Guidebooks, 12-14

hang yao (small boat, Bangkok), 110
Hakka women, 96
Hawaii, 159. *See also* Honolulu
Health, 11. *See also* Diseases; Immunizations
Heian Shrine (Kyoto), 38, 39-41
Holidays, 7
hondo (main hall, Buddhist temple), 40
Honolulu: USS *Arizona* memorial, 161; arrival, 159; food, 160, 162; getting around, 159; lodging, 162; sights, 160-161; snorkeling, 160. *See also* Hawaii
Hong Kong, 3, 4, 8, 9, 10; arrival, 78-79; description and history, 76-78; exchange rate, 8, 78-79; food, 9, 81-82; getting around, 81, 82, 83, 88-89; islands, 88-92; lodging, 79-81, 90; public transportation, 9, 79, 81, 82, 88-89; shopping, 82, 83, 84, 85, 86, 88, 96; sights, 84-87, 89-92, 93-97; tourist association, 78; visitor information, 83, 87
Hotels, reservations, 7. *See also* lodging in individual destinations
hutong (alleyway, China), 48, 50, 51

Immunizations, 11. *See also* Health
Imperial Palace (Kyoto), 32-33, 34, 36-37
Indonesia, 5, 6; exchange rate, 8, 130; guidebooks, 13; tourist information, 14, 141. *See also* Bali; Denpasar; Ubud; Yogyakarta

Index

Insurance, trip cancellation, 15
International date line, 21
Itinerary, 1, 2, 3-5, 16-20; airline routes, 5-6; best months, 10; extra stops, 159; options, 2; planning, 4, 6, 7, 10, 11, 14. *See also* Airfares; Airlines; Guidebooks, individual destinations; Trip

jaffles (sandwiches, Bali), 139
Japan, 8, 9; exchange rate, 8, 21; food, 9; guidebooks, 12, 13; language, 32; national holidays, 33; public transportation, 26; tourist information, 14. *See also* Kyoto
Japanese, basic vocabulary, 32
Jet lag, 28, 159

kaiseki (Kyoto-style dinner), 24
Kiyomizu Temple (Kyoto), 41-42
klong (canal, Thailand), 101
Koh Phangan, 126-127
Koh Samui: description and history, 122-123; food, 125; getting around, 123-124, 125-126; lodging, 124; sights, 126; snorkeling, 123. *See also* Bangkok; Thailand
Koh Tao, 126, 127
Kowloon, 76, 78, 82, 88
Kupu Kupu Barong, 148-149
Kuta (Bali), 151
Kyoto, 4; arrival, 21-22; application for visit to Imperial Palace, 32-33; description and history, 27-28; exchange rate, 8, 21; food, 24-26; getting around, 26; holidays, 33; language, 32; lodging, 23-24; nightlife, 31; public transportation, 26; shopping, 30-31, 42; sights, 28-31; 34-37, 38-43; tourist information center, 32. *See also* Japan

Lake Batur, 152-153
Lake Bratan, 147-148
Land Between tour, 93-97
Lantau, 90-92
lassis (yogurt drinks, Bali), 140
Legean (Bali), 151
Lodging, 8. *See also* individual destinations
losmen (homestays, Bali), 130

maiko (geisha's apprentice), 31
mai pen rai (it doesn't matter, Thailand), 100
Mas (Bali), 144
Master of Nets Garden (Suzhou), 71
merus (towers, Thailand), 136
Middle Kingdom, 4, 13, 44, 46, 53, 73
mie goreng (fried noodles, Thailand), 139
mingei (Japanese folk craft), 42-43
Ming Tombs, 52, 54
Money, 7-8; credit cards, 7; exchange rates, 8; inflation, 7-8; safety, 7; traveler's checks, 7. *See also* Exchange rates
Municipal Children's Palace (Shanghai), 74
Museum of Chinese History (Beijing), 55
Museum of the Chinese Revolution (Beijing), 55

nasi campur (steamed rice dinner, Bali), 140, 141
nasi putih (white rice, Bali), 141
Night Bazaar (Chiang Mai), 121-122
New Territories, 4, 76, 93

Opium War, 66, 77
Osaka, 21. *See also* Kyoto; Japan

Palace Museum (Beijing), 56
Passport, 10, 11, 12
People's Republic of China, 4, 8, 9, 10, 54; food, 9; visas, 10
Philosopher's Trail (Kyoto), 28, 29, 30
Phuket Coast, 3, 122
Phuping Palace, 121
prang (spire, Thailand), 110
Public transportation, 9-10. *See also* individual destinations
Pura Besakeh (Bali), 153
Pura Taman Ayun, 150
Puri Lukisan Museum (Bali), 135-136

renminbi (Chinese currency), 46
Royal Barges (Bangkok), 110-111

Safety, 7. *See also* Health
Sangeh (Bali), 146-147
sate, nasi goreng (fried rice, Bali), 139
Shanghai: arrival, 60; description and history, 61-62; food, 63; getting around, 65, 73; lodging, 62-63; nightlife, 64, 74-75; river cruise, 74; shopping, 68, 73, 75; sights, 66-68, 73-74. *See also* Beijing; China; Suzhou
Shanghai Museum of Art and History, 65, 68
Shek-O, 83, 87
Shijo Street (Kyoto), 27, 30-31
siheyuan (courtyard housing, Beijing), 50
Singaraja, 148
Snorkeling, 4, 5, 123, 148, 153, 155, 160

soba (noodle, Japan), 25
Summer Palace (Beijing), 4, 56, 58-59
Sun Yat-sen, 61
Suzhou, 4; arrival, 69; biking, 69, 72; description and history, 70; getting around, 69-70; shopping, 72; sights, 70-72. *See also* China; Shanghai

Tanah Lot (Bali), 149, 150
Temple of the Emerald Buddha (Bangkok), 104
Temples: Bali, 136, 146-147, 150, 152-153; Bangkok, 103-105, 110; Beijing, 57, 59, 60; Chiang Mai, 120-121; Hong Kong, 90, 91, 96; Koh Samui, 126; Kyoto, 28-30, 34-35, 39-42; Suzhou, 70; Ubud, 136-137; Yogyakarta, 158
Tenganan, 156
Thailand, 4, 8, 10; boxing, 106; customs, 99-100; description and history, 98-100; exchange rate, 8, 102; food, 9; guidebooks, 14; hill tribes, 118; islands, 122-127; language, 100; public transportation, 10, 102-103; tourist information, 14, 109, 116; weather, 98. *See also* Bangkok; Chiang Mai
Tian'anmen Square, 48, 52, 54-55
Tickets. *See* Airfares; Airlines
Ticket wholesalers, 6
Tirta Gangga, 157
Toilets, Western-style, 8, 22
Tourism Authority of Thailand, 116
Tourist information, 14
Travel agent, 6, 15
Traveler's checks, 7, 12

Trekking, 116, 119
Trip: cancellation insurance, 6, 15; clothing, 11; driving, 14; packing, 11; planning, 10, 14. *See also* Airfares; Airlines; Itinerary
tuk-tuk (motorized three-wheeler, Bangkok), 101

Ubud: arts and crafts, 134-136, 144; arrival, 130; dance, 137-138; description and history, 134; exchange rate, 8, 130; food, 138-141; getting around, 130, 142-143, 145-146; lodging, 130-133; shopping, 135, 144; sights, 134-138, 143-144. *See also* Bali

Ujung, 156-157

Vaccinations, 11. *See also* Health
Victoria Peak (Hong Kong), 83, 85
Visas, 10

Wangfujing Street (Beijing), 44, 48, 50-51, 55
warung (food concession, Bali), 1
Wat Arun, 110
Wat Chiang Man, 120
Wat Phra Keo, 104
Wat Phra Sing, 120
Wat Phrathat, 121
Water, safety of, 11
wayang kulit (puppet theater, Bali), 136

Yeh Pulu (Bali), 143-144
Yogyakarta (Java), 157-158
Yonghegong (Lama) Temple, 60

Zen Buddhism, 28, 40

Other Books from John Muir Publications

Adventure Vacations: From Trekking in New Guinea to Swimming in Siberia, Bangs 256 pp. $17.95

Asia Through the Back Door, 3rd ed., Steves and Gottberg 326 pp. $15.95

Belize: A Natural Destination, Mahler, Wotkyns, Schafer 304 pp. $16.95

Bus Touring: Charter Vacations, U.S.A., Warren with Bloch 168 pp. $9.95

California Public Gardens: A Visitor's Guide, Sigg 304 pp. $16.95

Catholic America: Self-Renewal Centers and Retreats, Christian-Meyer 325 pp. $13.95

Costa Rica: A Natural Destination, 2nd ed., Sheck 288 pp. $16.95

Elderhostels: The Students' Choice, 2nd ed., Hyman 312 pp. $15.95

Environmental Vacations: Volunteer Projects to Save the Planet, 2nd ed., Ocko 248 pp. $16.95

Europe 101: History & Art for the Traveler, 4th ed., Steves and Openshaw 372 pp. $15.95

Europe Through the Back Door, 10th ed., Steves 448 pp. $16.95

A Foreign Visitor's Guide to America, Baldwin and Levine 200 pp. $10.95 (avail. 9/92)

Floating Vacations: River, Lake, and Ocean Adventures, White 256 pp. $17.95

Great Cities of Eastern Europe, Rapoport 256 pp. $16.95

Gypsying After 40: A Guide to Adventure and Self-Discovery, Harris 264 pp. $14.95

The Heart of Jerusalem, Nellhaus 336 pp. $12.95

Indian America: A Traveler's Companion, 2nd ed., Eagle/Walking Turtle 448 pp. $17.95

Interior Furnishings Southwest: The Sourcebook of the Best Production Craftspeople, Deats and Villani 256 pp. $19.95 (avail. 9/92)

Mona Winks: Self-Guided Tours of Europe's Top Museums, Steves and Openshaw 456 pp. $14.95

Opera! The Guide to Western Europe's Great Houses, Zietz 296 pp. $18.95

Paintbrushes and Pistols: How the Taos Artists Sold the West, Taggett and Schwarz 280 pp. $17.95

The People's Guide to Mexico, 8th ed., Franz 608 pp. $17.95

The People's Guide to RV Camping in Mexico, Franz with Rogers 320 pp. $13.95

Ranch Vacations: The Complete Guide to Guest and Resort, Fly-Fishing, and Cross-Country Skiing Ranches, 2nd ed., Kilgore 396 pp. $18.95

The Shopper's Guide to Art and Crafts in the Hawaiian Islands, Schuchter 272 pp. $13.95

The Shopper's Guide to Mexico, Rogers and Rosa 224 pp. $9.95

Ski Tech's Guide to Equipment, Skiwear, and Accessories, ed. Tanler 144 pp. $11.95

Ski Tech's Guide to Maintenance and Repair, ed. Tanler 160 pp. $11.95

A Traveler's Guide to Asian Culture, Chambers 224 pp. $13.95

Traveler's Guide to Healing Centers and Retreats in North America, Rudee and Blease 240 pp. $17.95

Understanding Europeans, Miller 272 pp. $14.95

Undiscovered Islands of the Caribbean, 2nd ed., Willes 232 pp. $14.95

Undiscovered Islands of the Mediterranean, 2nd ed., Moyer and Willes 256 pp. $13.95

Undiscovered Islands of the U.S. and Canadian West Coast, Moyer and Willes 208 pp. $12.95

A Viewer's Guide to Art: A Glossary of Gods, People, and Creatures, Shaw and Warren 144 pp. $10.95

2 to 22 Days Series
Each title offers 22 flexible daily itineraries that can be used to get the most out of vacations of any length. Included are not only "must see" attractions but also little-known villages and hidden "jewels" as well as valuable general information.

22 Days Around the World, 1992 ed., Rapoport and Willes 256 pp. $12.95 (1993 ed. avail. 8/92)

2 to 22 Days Around the Great Lakes, 1992 ed., Schuchter 192 pp. $9.95

22 Days in Alaska, Lanier 128 pp. $7.95
2 to 22 Days in the American Southwest, 1992 ed., Harris 176 pp. $9.95
2 to 22 Days in Asia, 1992 ed., Rapoport and Willes 176 pp. $9.95 (**1993 ed.** avail. 8/92)
2 to 22 Days in Australia, 1992 ed., Gottberg 192 pp. $9.95 (**1993 ed.** avail. 8/92)
2 to 22 Days in California, 1992 ed., Rapoport 192 pp. $9.95 (**1993 ed.** avail. 8/92)
22 Days in China, Duke and Victor 144 pp. $7.95
2 to 22 Days in Europe, 1992 ed., Steves 276 pp. $12.95
2 to 22 Days in Florida, 1992 ed., Harris 192 pp. $9.95 (**1993 ed.** avail. 8/92)
2 to 22 Days in France, 1992 ed., Steves 192 pp. $9.95
2 to 22 Days in Germany, Austria, & Switzerland, 1992 ed., Steves 224 pp. $9.95
2 to 22 Days in Great Britain, 1992 ed., Steves 192 pp. $9.95
2 to 22 Days in Hawaii, 1992 ed., Schuchter 176 pp. $9.95 (**1993 ed.** avail. 8/92)
22 Days in India, Mathur 136 pp. $7.95
22 Days in Japan, Old 136 pp. $7.95
22 Days in Mexico, 2nd ed., Rogers and Rosa 128 pp. $7.95
2 to 22 Days in New England, 1992 ed., Wright 192 pp. $9.95
2 to 22 Days in New Zealand, 1992 ed., Schuchter 176 pp. $9.95 (**1993 ed.** avail. 8/92)
2 to 22 Days in Norway, Sweden, & Denmark, 1992 ed., Steves 192 pp. $9.95
2 to 22 Days in the Pacific Northwest, 1992 ed., Harris 192 pp. $9.95
2 to 22 Days in the Rockies, 1992 ed., Rapoport 176 pp. $9.95
2 to 22 Days in Spain & Portugal, 1992 ed., Steves 192 pp. $9.95
2 to 22 Days in Texas, 1992 ed., Harris 192 pp $9.95 (**1993 ed.** avail. 8/92)
2 to 22 Days in Thailand, 1992 ed., Richardson 176 pp. $9.95 (**1993 ed.** avail. 8/92)
22 Days in the West Indies, Morreale and Morreale 136 pp. $7.95

Parenting Series

Being a Father: Family, Work, and Self, *Mothering* Magazine 176 pp. $12.95
Preconception: A Woman's Guide to Preparing for Pregnancy and Parenthood, Aikey-Keller 232 pp. $14.95
Schooling at Home: Parents, Kids, and Learning, *Mothering* Magazine 264 pp. $14.95
Teens: A Fresh Look, *Mothering* Magazine 240 pp. $14.95

"Kidding Around" Travel Guides for Young Readers
Written for kids eight years of age and older.

Kidding Around Atlanta, Pedersen 64 pp. $9.95
Kidding Around Boston, Byers 64 pp. $9.95
Kidding Around Chicago, Davis 64 pp. $9.95
Kidding Around the Hawaiian Islands, Lovett 64 pp. $9.95
Kidding Around London, Lovett 64 pp. $9.95
Kidding Around Los Angeles, Cash 64 pp. $9.95
Kidding Around the National Parks of the Southwest, Lovett 108 pp. $12.95
Kidding Around New York City, Lovett 64 pp. $9.95
Kidding Around Paris, Clay 64 pp. $9.95
Kidding Around Philadelphia, Clay 64 pp. $9.95
Kidding Around San Diego, Luhrs 64 pp. $9.95
Kidding Around San Francisco, Zibart 64 pp. $9.95
Kidding Around Santa Fe, York 64 pp. $9.95
Kidding Around Seattle, Steves 64 pp. $9.95
Kidding Around Spain, Biggs 108 pp. $12.95
Kidding Around Washington, D.C., Pedersen 64 pp. $9.95

"Extremely Weird" Series for Young Readers
Written for kids eight years of age and older.

Extremely Weird Bats, Lovett 48 pp. $9.95
Extremely Weird Birds, Lovett 48 pp. $9.95
Extremely Weird Endangered Species, Lovett 48 pp. $9.95
Extremely Weird Fishes, Lovett 48 pp. $9.95
Extremely Weird Frogs, Lovett 48 pp. $9.95
Extremely Weird Primates, Lovett 48 pp. $9.95
Extremely Weird Reptiles, Lovett 48 pp. $9.95
Extremely Weird Spiders, Lovett 48 pp. $9.95

Masters of Motion Series
For kids eight years and older.

How to Drive an Indy Race Car, Rubel 48 pages $9.95 paper (avail. 8/92)
How to Fly a 747, Paulson 48 pages $9.95 (avail. 9/92)
How to Fly the Space Shuttle, Shorto 48 pages $9.95 paper (avail. 10/92)

Quill Hedgehog Adventures Series
Green fiction for kids. Written for kids eight years of age and older.

Quill's Adventures in the Great Beyond. Waddington-Feather 96 pp. $5.95
Quill's Adventures in Wasteland, Waddington-Feather 132 pp. $5.95
Quill's Adventures in Grozzieland, Waddington-Feather 132 pp. $5.95

X-ray Vision Series
For kids eight years and older.

Looking Inside Cartoon Animation, Schultz 48 pages $9.95 paper (avail. 9/92)
Looking Inside Sports Aerodynamics, Schultz 48 pages $9.95 paper (avail. 9/92)
Looking Inside the Brain, Schultz 48 pages $9.95 paper

Other Young Readers Titles

The Indian Way: Learning to Communicate with Mother Earth, McLain 114 pp. $9.95
The Kids' Environment Book: What's Awry and Why, Pedersen 192 pp. $13.95
Kids Explore America's Hispanic Heritage, Westridge Young Writers Workshop 112 pp. $7.95
Rads, Ergs, and Cheeseburgers: The Kids' Guide to Energy and the Environment, Yanda 108 pp. $12.95

Automotive Titles

How to Keep Your VW Alive, 14th ed., 440 pp. $21.95
How to Keep Your Subaru Alive 480 pp. $21.95
How to Keep Your Toyota Pickup Alive 392 pp. $21.95
How to Keep Your Datsun/Nissan Alive 544 pp. $21.95
The Greaseless Guide to Car Care Confidence: Take the Terror Out of Talking to Your Mechanic, Jackson 224 pp. $14.95
Off-Road Emergency Repair & Survival, Ristow 160 pp. $9.95

Ordering Information
If you cannot find our books in your local bookstore, you can order directly from us. Please check the "Available" date above. If you send us money for a book not yet available, we will hold your money until we can ship you the book. Your books will be sent to you via UPS (for U.S. destinations). UPS will not deliver to a P.O. Box; please give us a street address. Include $3.75 for the first item ordered and $.50 for each additional item to cover shipping and handling costs. For airmail within the U.S., enclose $4.00. All foreign orders will be shipped surface rate; please enclose $3.00 for the first item and $1.00 for each additional item. Please inquire about foreign airmail rates.

Method of Payment
Your order may be paid by check, money order, or credit card. We cannot be responsible for cash sent through the mail. All payments must be made in U.S. dollars drawn on a U.S. bank. Canadian postal money orders in U.S. dollars are acceptable. For VISA, MasterCard, or American Express orders, include your card number, expiration date, and your signature, or call (800) 888-7504. Books ordered on American Express cards can be shipped only to the billing address of the cardholder. Sorry, no C.O.D.'s. Residents of sunny New Mexico, add 5.875% tax to the total.

Address all orders and inquiries to:
John Muir Publications
P.O. Box 613
Santa Fe, NM 87504
(505) 982-4078
(800) 888-7504